FIRST AID IN ENGLISH

READER

by

ANGUS MACIVER

W0007140

BOOK
E

ROBERT GIBSON & SONS, Glasgow, LIMITED
17 FITZROY PLACE : : GLASGOW G3 7SF

P·A = No · 71/1

Books by
ANGUS MACIVER

FIRST AID IN ENGLISH
NEW FIRST AID IN ENGLISH

CONCISE FIRST AID IN ENGLISH
Edited by D.A. MacLennan, M.A.

READERS

READER A
READER B
READER C
READER D
READER E
READER F

**The information in this edition
is correct to May 1992.**

Copyright ANGUS MACIVER

© 1983

ISBN 0 7169 5504 0

Printed in Great Britain by Bell and Bain Ltd., Glasgow

PREFACE

In earlier stages of reading, emphasis has been placed on the mechanics of diction and the attainment of an adequate speed of recital. At this stage, the most important needs are to understand fully what is read and to acquire a taste for reading. To ensure the necessary concentration, **the stories in these books are specially selected to arouse, maintain, and satisfy the interest of the pupils.** The short paragraphs of Interesting Facts have a direct bearing on the stories, either by subject or scene, and should help considerably in the change from **learning to read** to **reading to learn.** The Questions on both Stories and Facts are **in sequence** and demand not only that the pupils read carefully but also that they remember the salient points. The answers (oral or written) can be used as **a direct aid to Composition.** The Development Exercises endeavour to expand on certain statements in the matter read, and the questions are designed to give the pupils an opportunity to express their thoughts and knowledge, simply and accurately.

These Readers are complementary to " First Aid in English," and therefore needless repetition, in language study and correct usage, has been purposely avoided.

A. M.

ACKNOWLEDGMENTS

We value highly the permission to include copyright material and are happy to put on record our indebtedness for:

THE MAGIC MIRROR
from *Forty More Tales*, by permission of Mr. Stephen Southwold.

SHIPS
by J.J. Bell, by permission of Mr. Adam L. Gowans.

THE CHRISTIANS TO THE LIONS
from *Beric the Briton*, by G.A. Henty,
by permission of Messrs Blackie & Son, Ltd.

KINDNESS REWARDED
adapted from *Legends of Greece and Rome*, by Grace A. Kupfer,
by permission of Messrs. George G. Harrap & Co. Ltd.

AN EXCITING ADVENTURE
adapted from 'Let her Rip'. Reprinted from *The Rover Book*,
by permission of Messrs. D.C. Thomson & Co. Ltd.,
London, Glasgow and Dundee.

THE BLUEBIRD AND THE INDIANS
adapted from *The Bluebird and the Indians*, by E.C. Matravers,
by permission of Messrs. Dean & Son, Ltd.

THE ADVENTURES OF TOM SAWYER
adapted from *The Adventures of Tom Sawyer*, by Mark Twain,
by permission of Messrs. Chatto & Windus.

SONG OF A BLUE MOUNTAIN STREAM
by Reginald Murray, by permission of the author.

We are also grateful to the Aluminium Federation, London, for information on bauxite and aluminium, and to Messrs. Prévité & Co. Ltd., Sevenoaks, for information on the Trinidad Asphalt Lake.

CONTENTS

THE OLD SEA-DOG

(*TREASURE ISLAND, by Robert Louis Stevenson, is one
of the most popular stories ever written.   The tale is
related by a boy—Jim Hawkins—and it is crammed with
exciting adventures—a stolen map—cruel and blood-
thirsty pirates—thrilling incidents on board the
" Hispaniola " while in quest of hidden treasure—the
discovery of untold wealth and the final victory over the
buccaneers.*)

I TAKE up my pen and go back to the time when my
father kept the " Admiral Benbow " Inn, and the
brown old seaman with the sabre-cut first took up his
lodging under our roof.

I remember him as if it was yesterday, as he came
plodding to the inn-door, his sea-chest following behind
him in a hand-barrow ; a tall, strong, heavy, nut-brown
man ; his tarry pigtail falling over the shoulders of his
soiled blue coat ; his hands ragged and scarred, with
black, broken nails ; and the sabre-cut across one cheek,
a dirty livid white.

I remember him looking round the cove and whistling
to himself as he did so, and then breaking out in that
old sea-song that he sang so often afterwards—

> *" Fifteen men on the dead man's chest—*
> *Yo-ho-ho and a bottle of rum,*
> *Drink and the devil had done for the rest—*
> *Yo-ho-ho and a bottle of rum."*

He rapped at the door with a bit of stick, and when my father appeared, called roughly for a glass of rum. This, when it was brought to him, he drank slowly, and kept looking about him at the cliffs and up at the signboard.

" This is a handy cove," says he at length, " and a pleasant grog-shop. Much company, mate ? "

My father told him no—very little company, the more was the pity.

" Well, then," said he, " this is the berth for me. Here you, matey," he cried to the man who trundled the barrow, " bring up alongside and help up my chest. I'll stay here a bit," he continued. " I'm a plain man ; rum and bacon and eggs is what I want, and that head up there, for to watch ships off. You may call me Captain. Oh! I see what you're at—there! " and he threw down three or four gold pieces on the threshold. " You can tell me when I've worked through that," says he, looking as fierce as a commander.

And indeed, bad as his clothes were, and coarsely as he spoke, he had none of the appearance of a man who had sailed before the mast ; but seemed like a mate or skipper. The man who came with the barrow told us the mail had set him down the morning before at the " Royal George," that he had enquired what inns there were along the coast, and hearing ours well spoken of, I suppose, and described as lonely, had

chosen it from the others as his place of residence.
And that was all we could learn of our guest.

He was a very silent man by custom. All day he
hung around the cove, or upon the cliffs, with a brass
telescope ; all evening he sat in a corner of the parlour
next the fire, and drank rum and water very strong.
Mostly he would not speak when spoken to ; only look
up sudden and fierce, and blow through his nose like
a fog-horn ; and we, and the people who came about
the house, soon learned to let him be. Every day when

he came back from his stroll, he would ask if any seafaring men had gone by along the road.

At first we thought it was the want of company of his own kind that made him ask this question ; but at last we began to see he was desirous to avoid them. When a seaman put up at the " Admiral Benbow," he would look in at him through the curtained door before he entered the parlour ; and he was always sure to be as silent as a mouse when any such was present. For me, at least, there was no secret about the matter, for I was, in a way, a sharer in his alarms.

He had taken me aside one day, and promised me a silver fourpenny on the first of every month, if I would only keep my " weather-eye open for a seafaring man with one leg," and let him know the moment he appeared. Often enough, when the first of the month came round, and I applied to him for my wage, he would only blow through his nose at me, and stare me down ; but before the week was out he was sure to think better of it, bring me my fourpenny piece, and repeat his orders to look out for " the seafaring man with one leg."

How that personage haunted my dreams, I need scarcely tell you. On stormy nights, when the wind shook the four corners of the house, and the surf roared along the cove and up the cliffs, I would see him in a thousand forms. To see him leap and run and pursue me over hedge and ditch, was the worst of nightmares. And altogether, I paid pretty dear for my monthly fourpenny piece in the shape of these fancies.

But, though I was so terrified by the idea of the seafaring man with one leg, I was far less afraid of the

Captain himself, than anybody else who knew him. There were nights when he took a deal more rum and water than his head could carry ; and then he would sometimes sit and sing his wicked, old, wild sea-songs, minding nobody ; but sometimes, he would force all the trembling company to listen to his stories, or bear a chorus to his singing.

Often I have heard the house shaking with " Yo-ho-ho, and a bottle of rum " ; all the neighbours joining in for dear life, with the fear of death upon them, and each singing louder than the other, to avoid remark. People were frightened at the time, but on looking back they rather liked it ; it was a fine excitement in a quiet country life ; and there was even a party of the younger men who pretended to admire him ; calling him a " true sea-dog " and a " real old salt," and such like names, and saying there was the sort of man that made England terrible at sea.

From " Treasure Island," by Robert Louis Stevenson.

INTERESTING FACTS
ABOUT
PIRATES.

1. **Pirates, corsairs, sea-rievers, filibusters, free-booters** and **sea-robbers** were the villains who plundered ships on the high seas. **Buccaneers** were originally hunters of wild cattle (French word—boucaniers) and they turned pirates, in seeking revenge upon the Spaniards. Later, they became a colony of freebooters, calling themselves " **The Brethren of the Coast.**"

2. In the earliest days of piracy, the sea-robbers flew the flag of their own country. Some time afterwards, the " **Jolly Roger** " was introduced, and this dreaded banner consisted of a black flag with a white skull and crossbones in the centre.

3. The old Norse pirates were called **Vikings** and they ravaged and plundered nearly every coast in Europe. These rievers settled in many of the places

which they raided, and formed colonies in such countries as Iceland, Greenland, and the British Isles.

4. At one time the richest prizes for pirates were the ships trading in the Mediterranean Sea. The notorious **Barbary Pirates** came from the Berber States—Tunis, Algeria, Morocco—along the north coast of Africa. Prisoners taken by them were held to ransom or sold as slaves.

5. The greatest hunting ground of the pirates was the "**Spanish Main**," a name given to the land lying along the north coast of South America. Here, and in other parts of the New World, the Spaniards forced the native Indians to give up all their wealth. The pirate ships lurked among the many islands of the Caribbean Sea, and tried to capture the Spanish galleons laden with treasure.

6. Pirate ships were generally very fast vessels, as they had to pursue and overtake their victims, and be able to escape from stronger enemies. Apart from the heavy iron and brass cannon on board, a pirate's

weapons consisted of the musket, pistol, dirk or dagger, and the cutlass (a heavy curved sword).

7. Pirates inflicted the most dreadful tortures on their prisoners. In " Walking the Plank," the victims were drowned by being compelled to walk on a plank, which was put out from the ship's side. In " Hanging from the Yard-arm," the prisoners were hanged from the high spars supporting the sails. The punishment of " Keel-hauling " meant dragging the captives from one side of the ship to the other under the keel.

8. When a ship was short of the necessary crew, a party was sent ashore to " Shanghai " men. They made men insensible by drink, drugs, or other methods, and when the victims recovered they found themselves far out at sea. The " Press Gang " was a party of sailors from a warship, who forced men to enlist in the navy.

9. " Davy Jones' Locker " was said to be the final resting-place of all sailors who were drowned at sea. The name " Jack Tar " is derived from the old habit of a sailor tarring his trousers to make them waterproof. The sailor's collar goes back to the days when seafaring men had greasy and tarry pigtails. The collar soon became dirty, but it was easily taken off and cleaned.

10. Doubloons, Pieces of Eight, Cross-money, Moidores, and Guineas are often mentioned in pirate

stories. A doubloon was a Spanish gold coin worth about £1·40. A piece of eight was a Spanish silver coin worth about 25p, and it is interesting to note that the sign for a dollar ($) was obtained from the figure 8 used on this coin. Pieces of metal, cross-marked by the priests to show that they were genuine pieces of gold, were called Cross-money. A moidore was a Portuguese gold coin worth about £1·35. A guinea was an English gold coin worth £1·05. It received that name because the first coins were made from gold brought from Guinea, in Africa.

QUESTIONS ON THE STORY.

1. From which famous story is this lesson taken?
2. Name the author.
3. What was the name of the Inn?
4. Who is the chief character in the lesson?
5. Describe in detail his appearance.
6. Where did he keep all his worldly possessions?
7. What other Inn is mentioned in the story?
8. Give as much as you can of the song.
9. Why did the Captain choose to stay at this particular Inn?
10. What advance payment for lodging did he make?
11. How did he pass the time during the day?
12. What did he take with him?
13. What question did he always ask on return from his daily strolls?
14. What happened when a seafarer put up at the Inn?
15. For whom was the boy told to keep a sharp look-out?
16. How much did the Captain promise to give the boy?
17. When was the reward to be paid to him?
18. What did the boy see in his nightmares?
19. What would the Captain sometimes force the company to do?
20. How did some of the younger folk describe him?

QUESTIONS ON THE INTERESTING FACTS.

1. Give four different words for a pirate.
2. Name and describe the pirate flag.
3. Who were the Vikings?
4. Where did the Barbary Pirates operate?
5. What was the most famous hunting ground of the pirates?
6. With what weapons were pirates usually equipped?
7. Name three tortures inflicted by pirates on their prisoners.
8. What was the Press Gang?
9. What is meant by "Davy Jones' Locker"?
10. Name four coins often mentioned in pirate stories.

DEVELOPMENT EXERCISES.

1. Point out on a map of the world:—
   (a) The Home of the Vikings, (b) The Barbary Coast, (c) The Spanish Main.
2. "Fifteen men on the dead man's chest" was an old sea-song. What is the special name given to a sea-song? Do you know any such songs? When did the sailors sing them?
3. The Captain had his sea-chest trundled along in a hand-barrow. Compare methods of modern road transport with those at the time of the story.
4. The Captain's hands were ragged and scarred and he had a sabre-cut across one cheek. How do you think he came by these marks?
5. Although it is very interesting and exciting to read about pirates, we do not admire them. Why not?
6. Now-a-days ships carrying valuable cargoes voyage from one part of the world to another without fear of being plundered. Can you give any reasons for this?
7. Compare a cargo ship of the time of the story with a present-day merchant ship.
8. Why are most sailors very interesting story-tellers? What do you understand by (a) a tall story, (b) a yarn, (c) a cock and bull story?

ALMOST A DISASTER

IN a wild part of Western Virginia in the United States of America, lived a poor old widow and her daughter. Their home was a tumble-down old shack, built near a great chasm, and miles away from any neighbours. The railway, which ran between Baltimore and Ohio, had its track close-by, and it spanned the yawning ravine by means of a high wooden bridge.

The winter had been bitterly cold and by far the most severe experienced in that particular district for many years. Early in the month of March, the snow on the mountain heights melted and formed roaring torrents, which rushed into the valleys below. The surging water rose higher and higher in the gorge, and the two women became alarmed when they saw that the bridge was in danger of being swept away.

One evening, the ceaseless roar seemed to be even louder than usual, and the old woman and her daughter went to bed feeling very uneasy in their minds, and wondering how long the bridge would resist the terrible swirling water. About midnight, the harsh noise of rending timber awakened them, and the startled frightened women quickly rose and dressed. Out into the howling wind they hurried to see what actual damage had been done, and to their horror they found that the bridge had been practically destroyed, and that a few hanging beams, and some broken twisted rails, were all that remained.

The old woman was quick to realise the awful danger —the night train from Baltimore to Ohio was due to cross the bridge in about half an hour. What could she do ? There was no signal-box, no telegraph station to which she could run in order to warn the fast approaching train of the danger ahead. In that howling wind, a shout would only be heard as a whisper. There was but one way of stopping the train, and that was to show a bright danger light. Clinging to each other for support, the two women stumbled back to the little shack in order to find some means of giving a warning signal.

The question of a light was a difficult one, as the glass globe of her only lamp had been accidentally broken a few days before, and the pile of wood, which she had gathered for the winter fires, was almost exhausted. True she had a few candles in the cupboard, but they were of no use, as the force of the wind would extinguish them the moment that they were exposed to the outside air. There must be some way of saving the train was the thought which flashed through her mind.

Her eyes roved anxiously round the little hut, and finally rested on the old bedstead, and the well-worn chairs. No—there was nothing else in the cabin which could provide sufficient light for a warning beacon. The younger woman seemed to read her mother's mind, for, with eager and trembling hands, she seized an axe, which lay in the corner, and

chopped the old bedstead until it was broken in pieces on the floor. The older woman gathered the bits of wood, and with a struggle, carried her load to the middle of the railway track. When she thought that the pile was large enough for her purpose, she tried to set it alight, but this was easier said than done, for match after match failed owing to the strong, blustery wind. The daughter then went back, and returning with the lamp, she poured the remaining paraffin oil on the broken splinters. Nestling close to each other, and shielding the flame, they at last succeeded in setting fire to the furniture.

The fire had no sooner begun to crackle and blaze than the distant rumble of the train was heard. Mother and daughter hoped and prayed that the engine-driver would see the warning light and stop the locomotive in time. Suddenly another idea struck the old woman—she remembered that she possessed a large

red cloth. Quickly she made her way to the hut, seized the cloth, and tied it to a piece of stick. Back to the track she hurried, and began waving her hastily-made flag in the light of the fire. Her daughter, not to be outdone, took hold of a burning ember and flourished it vigorously above her head.

Nearer and nearer came the train, and, when it rounded the curve a short distance in front of them, they could see the light of the engine become brighter and brighter. Both women now waved frantically, and to their great joy and relief, they heard the harsh grinding noise of the brakes. The train pulled up with a jolt and came to a standstill a few yards from the blazing pile.

A sudden sound of confusion and then all was hustle

and bustle aboard the train. The driver and several railway attendants alighted to discover the reason for the abrupt stop and immediately questioned the old woman and her daughter. By lantern-light, some of the party went to examine the extent of the damage to the bridge, and they were appalled by the sight of the wreckage and the raging torrent in the chasm. On their return, one of the passengers drew the party's attention to the now smouldering furniture, and, in answer to further questions, the two women related the whole story. The listeners were deeply moved as they recognised that this was an act of courageous self-sacrifice, and all decided that such bravery should not go unrewarded.

A few weeks later, the old woman and her daughter received the surprising and very welcome news that the Railway Company had decided to build them a little cottage, and that the passengers, who had been aboard the train on that fateful night, had subscribed a goodly sum of money, which would keep them in comfort for many a long day.

(Adapted.)

QUESTIONS ON THE STORY.

1. Where did the story take place?
2. Who are the principal characters?
3. In what kind of house did the women stay?
4. Name the towns between which the railway ran.
5. In what month did the floods rush into the valleys?
6. About what time did the mother and daughter hear a terrific din?
7. What did they do on hearing the noise?

8. Why were the women worried when they saw the wrecked bridge ?
9. Why was it difficult to warn the train ?
10. Name the articles of furniture mentioned in the story.
11. What did they decide to do in the circumstances ?
12. Why did their plan almost fail ?
13. What did the older woman do to attract the driver's attention ?
14. Not to be outdone, what did the daughter do ?
15. What happened when the train reached the spot ?
16. Who questioned the women as to why they had stopped the train ?
17. What made the search party shudder ?
18. How was the self-sacrifice of the women discovered ?
19. What reward did the Railway Company give to the couple ?
20. How did the passengers show appreciation of their bravery ?

WOODEN BRIDGE

SINGLE SPAN STONE

DRAWBRIDGE

STONE ARCHED

COMMON TRUSS

ARCHED BEAM

LATTICE BRIDGE

DECK BRIDGE

SWING BRIDGE

SUSPENSION

CANTILEVER

BASCULE BRIDGE

1. These drawings illustrate the principle of a particular type of bridge shown on the previous page.

Which type?

2. Can you give illustrations of any others ?

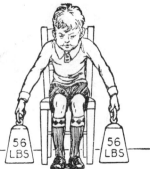

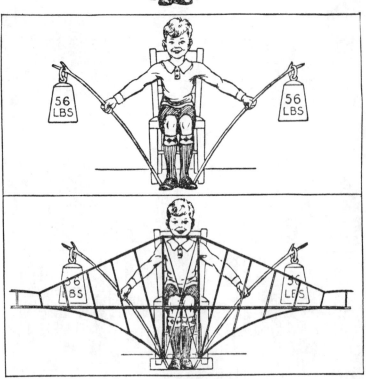

PAID IN HIS OWN COIN

[*When Muhammad (or Mahomet) the Great Prophet died, the Arabs entrusted the spiritual power of their religion to the Caliphs. The following story illustrates the wisdom of the Caliph Haroun-al-Raschid, who was known as the " Solomon of the Arabs." So that you will understand the story better, here are the meanings of certain uncommon words which appear in the lesson:—BEY—a governor, AGA—a commander or lord, CADI—a local judge, MUFTI— a law official, KORAN—the Muslim Scriptures upon which Arab Law is based.*]

IN the reign of Caliph Haroun-al-Raschid, of happy memory, there lived in the city of Baghdad a celebrated barber of the name of Ali Sakal. He was famous for a steady hand and so dexterous in his profession was he, that he could shave a head or trim a beard and whiskers with his eyes blindfolded, without once drawing blood.

There was not a man of any fashion in Baghdad who did not employ him; and such a run of business had he, that at last he became proud and insolent, and would scarcely ever touch a head whose master was not at least a bey or an aga.

25

Wood for fuel was always scarce and dear in Baghdad, and, as his shop consumed a great deal, the wood-cutters brought their loads to him in preference, almost sure of meeting with a ready sale.

It happened one day that a poor wood-cutter, new in his profession, and ignorant of the character of Al Sakal, went to his shop and offered him for sale a load of wood, which he had just brought from a considerable distance in the country on his donkey. Ali immediately offered him a price, making use of these words, " For all the wood that is upon the donkey."

The wood-cutter agreed, unloaded his beast, and asked for the money. " You have not given me all the wood yet," said the barber ; " I must have the pack-saddle " (which is chiefly made of wood) " into the bargain—that was our agreement." " How ? " said the other in great amazement, " who ever heard of such a bargain ? It is impossible."

In short, after many words and much argument, the overbearing barber seized the pack-saddle, wood and all, and sent away the poor peasant in great distress. He immediately ran to the cadi and stated his grievance. The cadi was one of the barber's customers and refused to hear the case.

The wood-cutter went to a higher judge. He also patronised Ali Sakal and made light of the complaint. The poor man then appealed to the mufti, who, having pondered over the question, at length settled that it was too difficult a case for him to decide, no provision being made for it in the Koran ; and therefore the peasant must put up with his loss.

The wood-cutter was not disheartened, but forthwith got a scribe to write a petition to the Caliph himself, which was duly presented on Friday, the day when he went in state to the mosque. The Caliph's punctuality in reading petitions was well known, and it was not long before the wood-cutter was called to his presence.

When he had approached the Caliph, he knelt and kissed the ground ; and then placing his arms straight before him, his hands covered with the sleeves of his cloak and his feet close together, he awaited the decision of his case.

" Friend," said the Caliph, " the barber has words on his side—you have the spirit of justice on yours. The law must be defined by words, and agreements must be made in words ; the former must have its course or it is nothing, and agreements must be kept, or there would be no faith between man and man ; therefore the barber must keep all his wood." Then calling the wood-cutter close to him, the Caliph whispered something in his ear, which none but he could hear, and sent him away quite satisfied.

The wood-cutter having made his bows of reverence, returned to his donkey, which was tied without, and proceeded to his home. A few days later, he applied to the barber, as if nothing had happened between them, requesting that he and a companion of his from the country might enjoy the dexterity of his hand ; and the price at which both operations were to be performed was settled.

When the wood-cutter's crown had been properly shorn, Ali Sakal asked where his companion was.

27

"He is just standing without here," said the other, "and he shall come in presently."

Accordingly he went out and returned, leading his donkey after him by the halter.

"This is my companion," said he, "and you must shave him."

"Shave him!" exclaimed the barber in the greatest surprise. "It is enough that I have consented to lower myself by touching you ; and do you dare to insult me by asking me to shave your donkey ? Away with you or I'll send you both to Jericho!" And forthwith he drove them out of his shop.

The wood-cutter immediately went to the Caliph, was admitted to his presence, and related his case.

"'Tis well," said the Commander of the Faithful. "Bring Ali Sakal and his razors to me this instant!" he exclaimed to one of his officers ; and in the course of ten minutes the barber stood before him.

"Why do you refuse to shave this man's companion ? " said the Caliph to the barber. "Was not that your agreement ? "

Ali, kissing the ground, answered, "'Tis true, O Caliph, that such was our agreement ; but who ever made a companion of a donkey before or who ever thought of treating it as a true believer ? "

"You may say right," said the Caliph ; "but at the same time, who ever thought of insisting on a pack-saddle being included in a load of wood ? No, no, it is the wood-cutter's turn now. To the donkey immediately, or you know the consequences."

The barber was then obliged to prepare a large
quantity of soap, to lather the beast from head to foot,
and to shave him in the presence of the Caliph and the
whole court, whilst he was jeered and mocked by the
taunts of the by-standers. The poor wood-cutter was
dismissed with a present of money, and all Baghdad
resounded with the story, and celebrated the justice of
the Commander of the Faithful.

From " Hajji Baba of Ispahan," by James Morier.

INTERESTING FACTS
ABOUT
THE ARABS.

1. The Arabs are an ancient race descended from the desert tribes of Arabia. They are natural wanderers and continually move about from one place to another. Some have settled in the villages and towns of Arabia, Palestine, Turkey, and along the north coast of Africa from Egypt to Morocco. In the last-named country they are known as **Moors**.

2. Religion plays a very large part in the life of the Arab. Followers of **Islam** worship God and regard

Mahomet as His Prophet. Each day, at dawn and sunset, the **muezzins** (criers) stand on the minarets of the **mosques** (churches) and call the Muslims to prayer. They kneel down facing **Mecca** (the holy town of their religion), and recite parts of their Bible. Outside the mosques may be seen rows and rows of sandals, as footwear is forbidden in places of worship.

3. The Bible of the Arabs is called the **Koran**, and it means both law

30

and religion to them. Mahomet claimed that God had come to him in visions, and so his utterances were recorded and considered sacred. In 622 A.D. the Arabs, who worshipped age-old tribal gods, made many attempts upon the prophet's life and he was forced to flee from Mecca to Medina. This flight is known as the **Hegira**, and it marks the beginning of the Arab calendar. Thus the Muslim date is 622 years less than the date on the Christian calendar. Friday is held as the Sabbath Day.

4. In Northern India, Afghanistan, Iran, Iraq, Turkey, Egypt, and Northern Africa there are many Muslims and each follower tries to make a pilgrimage to Mecca at least once in his life. On his return from the holy city, the pilgrim is allowed to wear a green turban, dye his beard red, and attach the honourable title of **Hajji** to his name.

5. The Arab dresses in a loose, flowing robe called **a burnous**, and on his head he binds a scarf, which protects him from the heat of the sun. The Arab woman is similarly dressed, but she wears a veil called a **yashmak**, which covers the lower half of her face.

6. Many Arabs still lead a wandering life in the desert, travelling from one oasis to another. An **oasis** is a fertile place where food and water can be obtained. These desert Arabs journey by camel, live in a cluster of tents called a **dowar**, eat dates mostly, and carry their water supply in large goatskin bottles.

7. To eat **salt** with Arabs is a mark of sincere friendship and means safety and protection while in their company. They always wash and pray before every meal. As is general throughout the East, the Arabs squat on the floor and eat from a central dish, using only their right hands to carry the food to their mouths. At the end of the meal everyone exclaims, " God be praised! " and then they all rise and proceed to wash their hands again.

8. In olden times, the Arab merchants brought their goods by **caravan** from such distant lands as China, India, Spain, and Central Africa, and sold them in their own markets or bazaars. In Arab towns, trading has been carried on in the same fashion for centuries.

When buying or selling they argue loud and long about the price. There are no shop windows as the goods are generally displayed on stalls, and members of the same trade are often grouped together in the same quarter of the town. Baghdad (the town in the story) was a famous trading centre, as it was at the cross-roads of many caravan routes, and was also a shipping port.

9. Although motor cars are now quite common in Arabia, horses and camels have always been the favourite methods of transport. Most Arabs are fine horsemen, and the Arab steed, swift and strong, is the horse from which the modern racehorse has been bred. The useful camel, known as " **The Ship of the Desert**," can travel for long distances without food or water and is the chief beast of burden in the country.

10. In early times, the Arabs ranked as one of the most important races in the world. They were a clever, intelligent people, and were keenly interested in **mathematics, chemistry,** and **astronomy.** Our present system of numbers (0, 1, 2, 3, 4, 5, 6, 7, 8, 9) was derived from Arab figures.

DROMEDARY

BACTRIAN CAMEL

QUESTIONS ON THE STORY.

1. In what city did the story take place ?
2. What was the barber's name ?
3. What proof is given to show his skill as a barber ?
4. How did his success in business affect him ?
5. From where did the poor wood-cutter bring the load of wood ?
6. How did the barber deceive him ?
7. To whom did the wood-cutter first state his grievance ?
8. What answer did he receive and why ?
9. What did the second judge (the mufti) say to his appeal ?
10. To whom did he send a petition ?
11. On which day was his petition presented ?
12. Describe the wood-cutter's actions in the mosque ?
13. What was the Caliph's reply ?
14. How did the wood-cutter deceive the barber ?
15. What did the poor man do to obtain justice ?
16. What orders did the Caliph give to his officers ?
17. Give the barber's reasons for not shaving the donkey ?
18. State the Caliph's answer and decision.
19. How did the by-standers behave ?
20. What other name was given to the Caliph ?

QUESTIONS ON THE INTERESTING FACTS.

1. In what countries are Arabs generally to be found ?
2. (a) Name their great prophet.
   (b) Where was he born ?
3. (a) What is the name given to the Bible of the Arabs ?
   (b) When are the Muslims called to prayer ?
   (c) Which day is held as the Sabbath Day ?
4. (a) What does each follower of Islam try to do at least once in his life ?
   (b) How may a pilgrim indicate that he has performed this sacred duty ?
5. Describe typical Arab dress.
6. (a) What is the name given to a group of Arab tents ?
   (b) How do the desert Arabs carry their drinking water ?

7. (a) What is a mark of sincere friendship with Arabs ?
   (b) Describe how they would eat a meal.
8. (a) Name a famous Arab trading centre of olden times.
   (b) Why was this town so important ?
9. Describe various methods of transport seen in Arabia.
10. In what branches of learning were the Arabs very interested ?

DEVELOPMENT EXERCISES.

1. Point out on the map the countries in which many Arabs live.
2. At the time of the story, wood was the most popular form of fuel. What are the chief kinds of fuel to-day ?
3. The Caliph was known as the " Solomon of the Arabs." What did this mean ? Can you remember any Bible story about Solomon ?
4. What is (a) an eastern caravan, (b) a modern caravan ? The Arab merchants brought their goods by caravan from such distant lands as China, India, Spain, and Central Africa. Why did they travel by caravan ? Name some of the goods likely to be brought from each of these countries.
5. Horses and camels are the favourite methods of transport in Arabia. How many other beasts of burden can you name ? In what countries are they used ?
6. Ali Sakal was a barber. What instruments are used in a modern hairdresser's shop ? What peculiar sign is to be seen outside the shop ?
7. The wood-cutter sold his wood in the streets of Baghdad. What things are commonly sold in our streets to-day ?
8. Desert Arab tribes are continually moving about from place to place. Why ? Describe an oasis.

THE DAFFODILS

I WANDERED lonely as a cloud
  That floats on high o'er vales and hills,
When all at once I saw a crowd,
A host, of golden daffodils ;
Beside the lake, beneath the trees,
Fluttering and dancing in the breeze.

Continuous as the stars that shine
And twinkle on the Milky Way,
They stretched in never-ending line
Along the margin of a bay ;
Ten thousand saw I at a glance
Tossing their heads in sprightly dance.

The waves beside them danced ; but they
Out-did the sparkling waves in glee :
A poet could not but be gay,
In such a jocund company ;
I gazed—and gazed—but little thought
What wealth the show to me had brought ;

For oft, when on my couch I lie
In vacant or in pensive mood,
They flash upon that inward eye
Which is the bliss of solitude ;
And then my heart with pleasure fills
And dances with the daffodils.

William Wordsworth.

THE MAGIC MIRROR

[The following story (not a true one) is very cleverly written and makes interesting reading. It points out a moral which we should all bear in mind.]

KING BARDOLPH was probably the most handsome monarch who had ever ruled over the fine and prosperous country of Carsovia. He was tall, and dark, and broad, and upright. His black hair was thick and curly, his eyes blue, his teeth white, his complexion ruddy, and his strong legs were as straight as fir trees.

In his throne-room, facing the throne, was a very bright, clear mirror ; and although he was by no means vain, King Bardolph would often stand in front of this mirror, and regard, with much satisfaction, his very comely reflection.

But as the years rolled on the King grew lazy. He gave up his hunting, and his riding ; he walked no more ; he breakfasted in bed, and then turned over and took a nap until noon. When he *did* go out, he lolled back in his fine carriage, and yawned.

After leading this indolent life for some time, King Bardolph came one morning, and stood before his splendid mirror. As he gazed at his reflection, he started back with horror. What could be wrong with the mirror ? Looking back at him from its smooth,

38

polished surface was a fat, blotchy, red-faced man with puffy eyes, a mottled nose, and a rounded stomach.

"Bless my buttons!" gasped Bardolph, "what a horrid-looking fellow! The mirror must be bewitched, for I'm sure that can't be *me*. I may be a trifle plump, but that creature is hideously fat, and certainly eats too much. Now, I don't eat too much. Let me see, what did I have for breakfast? Dear, dear, dear, what *was* it now? Er—six eggs, seven sausages, half a chicken, four rolls, some butter, some honey, and a couple of flagons of canary wine. Now *that's* not too much for a king. No, it certainly can *not* be me. Some wizard has bewitched the thing." And pulling a little doubtfully at his lips, he rang a bell.

When a footman entered, King Bardolph said, "Take this mirror up to the store-room, and bring another to put in its place."

After breakfast next morning, the King strolled over to the new mirror, and looked eagerly in it. To his anger and surprise, the same unwholesome fat-looking personage stared back at him.

Bardolph rang the bell furiously, and, when the footman entered timidly, he roared, "Take this mirror away, and see that a good one is in its place by morning."

Upon the morrow, King Bardolph hurried over his breakfast, and then walked up to the new mirror, as quickly as his breathlessness would allow. As he saw the same horrid-looking fellow gazing back at him, he raised his clenched fists above his head and bellowed madly.

At that moment, Diplo, his wisest and most trusted

counsellor, entered the throne-room. The King beckoned him, and when he had reached the mirror, King Bardolph said, pointing at the image in the glass, " Diplo, is that me ? "

" Is that I, Your Majesty means," ventured Diplo.

The King stared at him in angry puzzlement for a moment, and then he smiled and said, " Yes, of course, my wise Diplo, but kings make their own grammar. What I wish to know is — — Am I like *that* ? " And he flicked an impatient finger towards the mirror.

Diplo smiled. " Certainly not, Your Majesty," he replied.

" Then what in the name of thunder is the matter with the thing ? " asked the angry monarch.

" The glass is faulty," replied Diplo. " Come with me, Your Majesty," he continued ; and taking the King by the arm, he led him to a little window in the topmost turret of the palace.

Diplo pointed out over the blue distant hills. " Over there, O King," he said, " the sorcerer Mohrab, in the long ago, hid the Mirror of Truth. The man who wishes to see himself as he really is, must seek this magic mirror himself, and having found it, may look within and learn the truth."

" I will set off in my carriage to-morrow, after breakfast," said Bardolph.

" That would be useless," replied Diplo. " He who seeks the mirror of Truth must seek it afoot. Moreover," went on Diplo, " it is only to be found one hour after dawn. Thereafter, for the remainder of the day and night, it is invisible."

The King sighed deeply. " Ah, well," he said presently, " what must be, must be. To-morrow I will arise betimes and seek this magic glass."

And so, upon the morrow, King Bardolph arose from his silken bed before dawn, and upon unaccustomed feet searched the hills. But he sought in vain, and returned wearily homeward.

Diplo met him and said, " Do not lose heart, O King ; you will find, if you seek well : try again." And so upon the morrow, and for many morrows, for weeks indeed, and months, King Bardolph sought and sought among the distant hills, in the fresh cool dawns for the magic mirror. At the end of six months he was once again fine, slim, handsome, straight and ruddy.

Diplo came to him and said, " Your Majesty, I dreamed a dream last night, and in it I thought that the sorcerer Mohrab came to me and told me where the Mirror of Truth lies hidden. To-morrow I shall come with you and show you the place."

And so upon the morrow the two set off together. Diplo found it difficult to keep pace with the King's swift strides, but at last they reached the hills, just as the red face of the sun climbed over the misty peaks. The King stood staring at the beauty of the dawn, and seemed to have forgotten his errand, forgotten Diplo, forgotten everything.

A cry from the ground startled him to awareness. He looked down and there at his feet crouched Diplo, pulling from under the bushes a fine shining mirror. Diplo sprang to his feet, and crying triumphantly, " The Mirror of Truth ! " held it in front of the King.

The King stared into its smooth polished surface. He saw within it the loveliness of the eastern sky, and the splendour of the newcome sun. But he saw also a fine, handsome face, with ruddy complexion and crisp, curly, black hair.

"At last!" he cried, "the Mirror of Truth. I *knew* I was like that." Then, taking the mirror from Diplo, he turned it round and looked at its back. In the middle of the ebony was a long, jagged scratch.

King Bardolph looked wonderingly at the scratch for a long time, and then he said slowly, "Why, Diplo, my old mirror had a scratch on its back like that."

Diplo laughed softly. "No doubt, Your Majesty," he said ; and then after a little pause he went on, "for this *is* your old mirror."

" Then how in the name of legs did it get here ? " asked the astonished King.

" I got it from the store-room before we started," replied Diplo, " and carried it here under my cloak."

" You sly dog ! " cried Bardolph, not knowing whether to be angry or to laugh. " Then there is no such thing as a Mirror of Truth ? "

" On the contrary, Your Majesty," replied Diplo with a wise smile, " all mirrors are Mirrors of Truth ; and all mirrors now will show you the same reflection as the one you are holding."

" Diplo," said the King, as they made their way back to the palace, " you deserve a reward for your cleverness. What shall it be ? "

" A walk with Your Majesty," replied Diplo, " to the hills each dawn, as long as we both shall live."

" Granted ! " cried King Bardolph with a great laugh.

From " Forty More Tales," by Stephen Southwold.

THE INDIANS AND THE BLUE BIRD
(Founded on Fact)

(In the days of this story there was no " short- cut " such as the Panama Canal, and all ships, sailing from Europe to the west coast of America, crossed the Atlantic, rounded Cape Horn at the tip of South America, and then proceeded northwards along the coast until they reached their destination. This was a long and hazardous journey and generally took several months to complete.)

IT WAS in the year 1860 that I made my first voyage, having joined the crew of the sailing ship " Termagant," a large three-masted schooner, bound from London for the port of San Francisco on the west coast of the United States. Owing to a spell of calm weather, the first part of the trip across the Atlantic took much longer than expected, and by the time we had reached the " Roaring Forties," and rounded " The Horn," we had run very short of provisions. In some miraculous way, the cook managed, by strict rationing, to make what little food we had, last until the ship was within a few days' sailing distance of 'Frisco. At this point, however, there was not a scrap of food left in the larder, and in order to obtain something to eat, a few members of the crew landed early

44

each evening on the neighbouring coast to shoot the various water-fowl, which were plentiful in that region. I was the youngest of the hands, and had been advised not to wander far from the others on these expeditions, as the native Indian tribes were said to be unfriendly to white people.

One evening, having gone ashore just before sunset, I was attracted by a passing blue bird of remarkable beauty. It flew further inland towards a forest, and I immediately set off in hot pursuit. At last, when near enough to take aim, I shot, and to my intense delight, saw it fall straight to earth. In order to reach the bird, I had to make my way round a marsh on the edge of the wood, but eventually I secured my prize and slung it over my shoulder. As you may well imagine, I was very pleased with myself, for this particular bird was a fine specimen, much bigger than any bird caught previously, and certain to provide a welcome and tasty meal on board ship.

Soon after, I spotted a flock of birds in the distance, apparently of the same kind as I had shot, and, regardless of the consequences, I headed quickly in their direction. When I was near enough to shoot, it was too dark to aim accurately and I only succeeded in startling the birds. They flew quickly towards the forest uttering their weird cries. In my eagerness to obtain another bird, I followed, and fired my last remaining cartridges at them, but with no success.

It was only on giving up the chase that I realised how dark it had become, and that I had travelled a considerable distance from the shore without noticing the

direction I had taken. I looked up for guidance from
the stars, when, behold! I saw a pair of eyes gazing
down at mine.

There, close to me, lying along the branch of a tree,
was an Indian. When I moved away I saw others
hidden behind bushes or tree-trunks and pointing their
arrows at me. I at once determined to make a wide
curve to avoid these gentry ; but wherever I turned,
I found my way was cut off unless I went deeper into
the forest. On I scrambled, making repeated efforts
to turn right or left, but always finding myself faced
by an Indian with pointed arrow. In one last desperate
attempt, I dashed fully twenty yards but I was pulled
up by an arrow, which whished dangerously close and
struck a tree directly in my line of flight. I halted
abruptly, changed my course, and, with a few more steps,
suddenly came upon an Indian encampment with its
wigwams, squaws, and camp fires.

It became plain to me then, that I was trapped and in the power of a tribe of Indians. My pursuers closed round me and conducted me to the tent of one whom I supposed to be the chief. Several of them mounted guard over me, and the others went into the wigwam chatting eagerly, as I imagined, over my fate. Their voices grew louder and louder, until at last, one gave a sharp word of command and silence followed.

The chief, in long feathered head-dress, came out and approached me, and I noticed, by the light of the fire, that on the front of his leather tunic there was a fine embroidered design of just such a bird as I carried slung over my shoulder. The design was worked with dyed porcupine quills and various coloured threads.

My offence at once dawned on me. I had slain the totem, or the creature specially sacred to this tribe. I searched my memory to recall what fate awaited such an evil-doer. Would they burn me to death, or bury me alive, or chop me to pieces ? I looked with horror at the carefully plaited scalp-locks which adorned the chief's war club. Would mine soon be amongst them ?

Suddenly a strangely-attired creature, decked in a variety of skins and feathers, appeared and at once took command of the situation. What strange barbaric feast or sacrifice was being prepared, and the part I should be called upon to play in it, I could not guess. Great logs of wood were hurled on the fire till the flames leaped high in the dark night. To add to the general excitement, the drums were beaten and the women set up a dismal wail.

This scene continued for at least half an hour. Then a young brave, uttering a wild cry, leapt in my direction, at the same time swinging a heavy club. Truth to tell, I thought my last hour had come. Instead of striking me as I expected, he began to dance round me, making frightful faces and gestures. As he swayed and swept hither and thither, he seemed carried away by a frenzy of wild feeling.

After some moments, this jumping performer was joined by another, and they swept and revolved round me, their faces rapt with excitement ; but they never touched each other or me. Another short interval and three more men joined them ; then more and more, until I was the centre of a bewildering circle of dancers.

The women, meanwhile, were preparing some hot

and very intoxicating drink, of which the men took gulps
from time to time. The drums continued to boom and
thunder with ever quickening beat, and the wailing of
the women could be heard above the din.

After some considerable time, an idea flashed into my
mind. The blue bird, which was still hanging round
my shoulder, might be the centre of attraction. Was
it possible that this fine show was in honour of its death,
and was I a mere trifle, a beast of burden carrying a
sacred idol ? I determined to put my theory to the
test. I raised my hands, loosened the string, laid the
bird down at my feet, and then, thinking it the best
policy to startle the Indians, I leapt high in the air,
and to the tune of " Auld Lang Syne," which I sang at
the top of my voice, I began to dance a Highland Fling,
of which I had a vague remembrance.

The more sober and the less excited of the Indians
watched me carefully, but the greater number continued
their wild dance. At first I jigged and wheeled about in
a small circle, and then by degrees I widened it, the hope
of freedom springing in my heart. On and on I danced,
getting further and further from the fire and the chief's
tent. Occasionally a fierce glance terrified me, and a
club swung in my direction, but I was now quite certain
that the blue bird was the reason for this fantastic
ceremony.

Ten minutes later, I had danced to the outer edge of
the Indians, and was looking about anxiously for an
avenue of escape. Selecting a broad footpath, I waited
my opportunity, and then dashed off as fast as I could.
Soon, I was crashing my way through the dark forest,

fearful lest the Red men would pursue and recapture me.

Fortunately, by the time day had dawned, I had regained the coast, and saw the ship at anchor in the bay. My absence had been noted and it was not long before I fell in with the search-party sent to my assistance. Once more, saved despite my rashness, I set sail on the good ship " Termagant."

From " The Blue Bird and the Indians,"
by E. C. Matravers.

INTERESTING FACTS
ABOUT
THE RED INDIANS.

1. The Red Indian tribes were the original natives of North America and they roamed about in freedom until the white settlers from Europe arrived and made their homes there. Since the occupation of the land by the " **Palefaces**," they have lived in special allotted territories called **Reservations**.

2. The chief hunting tribes were the **Apache**, **Blackfeet**, **Cherokees**, **Crees**, **Iroquois**, **Mohawk**, **Navaho**, and **Sioux**.

The **Pawnee** and **Pueblo** tribes were noted for farming, and the **Hopi** tribe was famous for the making of baskets, carpets, and pottery.

3. The Indians wore leggings and moccasins of antelope skin, and adorned their heads with eagle feathers. In winter, they added a loose mantle of bison skin. The wife or **squaw** wore a long, belted, skin robe,

51

and carried her baby or **papoose** strapped to her back.

4. The following were the four chief types of dwellings used by the various tribes :—

- (*a*) The **wigwam** was a tent hung with bark and hides and shaped like a bee-hive.
- (*b*) The **tepee** was a pointed tent made of skins wrapped round a few poles.
- (*c*) The **long house** was a large wooden hut.
- (*d*) The **pueblo** was a peculiar stone and clay building of terraced houses with doorways in their flat roofs. Ladders were laid against the walls and these were drawn up when an enemy attacked them.

5. The Red men were cunning hunters and clever trackers. The old warriors taught the young boys, so that, at an early age, they became skilful with bow and arrow, and expert at paddling their frail canoes in dangerous streams and rapids. Their food consisted chiefly of deer and buffalo meat, and some tribes grew

corn and potatoes. **Wampum** (ornamental beads made from shells) was widely used as money.

6. The Indians possessed a high order of intelligence and from them we have learned the use of such things as moccasins, snowshoes, toboggans, hammocks, tobacco, and potatoes. They did not write their language in letters as we do, but made little drawings and painted pictures on the skins of their tepees and wigwams.

7. From early childhood Red Indians were taught to endure pain and suffering without crying, and they seldom showed signs of joy and happiness. They believed magic powers to be present in the sun, moon, and stars, and the " **medicine man** " (witch-doctor) was supposed to be able to control these powers. All Indian festivals were called **dances**, and only the men took an active part in them. They painted themselves in very bright colours, and danced wildly round their fires, calling loudly for supernatural aid to ensure food supplies for the future.

8. The North American Indians had a very strict code of honour and pride amongst themselves, and severely punished anyone who broke the tribal laws. The carved **totem poles**, with their peculiar designs, were thought to protect them from danger and hunger, and they were held sacred. The **calumet** or "**Pipe of Peace**," smoked and passed round as a token of friendship, was a long pipe adorned with plaited hair and feathers. The "**Happy Hunting Ground**" of the Indian was the paradise in which he expected to live after death.

9. Long before we had invented the Morse Code with its dots and dashes, the Indians used smoke signals to send messages. They often raided the settlements of the early pioneers and ambushed the **covered waggons** on the trail. When the Red Indian tribes were "on the warpath," they

fought with great cunning, and inflicted terrible tortures on their helpless captives. The warriors or " **braves** " took their victims' scalps to display as a sign of their courage and daring in battle. Their weapons were the tomahawk, club, flint-knife, and bow and arrow.

10. Daniel Boone was a famous hunter and trapper who acted as a scout and guide to many of the early settlers. " **Buffalo Bill** " was the popular name given to William Cody, a rider with the Overland Express Company. He received this title because he supplied buffalo meat to workmen who were constructing a railway. Buffalo Bill was also a scout with the United States Army and took part in many expeditions against the Indians.

QUESTIONS ON THE STORY.

1. What three words are used to tell you that it is a true story?
2. In what year did it happen?
3. Name the ship.
4. For which port was she bound?
5. Give the route taken by ships in those days.
6. What caused them to run short of provisions?
7. How did the crew obtain food?
8. What prize did the writer secure one evening?
9. What did he do with it?
10. What caused him to stray towards the forest?
11. Who chased and surrounded him?
12. What did he come upon in the heart of the forest?
13. What peculiar design had the chief on his leather tunic?
14. What punishment did he expect to receive?
15. Describe the scene round the camp-fire.
16. What idea flashed suddenly through his mind?
17. What song did he sing?
18. What dance did he try to do?
19. When did he reach the coast after his escape?
20. Who came to his assistance?

QUESTIONS ON THE INTERESTING FACTS.

1. (a) Give a Red Indian name for white people.
   (b) What is the name given to the special territories in which Red people live ?

2. Name five famous Red Indian tribes.

3. What are the following called ?—(a) a Red Indian wife, (b) a Red Indian baby.

4. Name three types of Red Indian dwellings.

5. What was wampum ?

6. Name some of the things which the Red Indians taught us to use.

7. (a) Who was the " medicine man " ?
   (b) Describe a Red Indian festival or dance.

8. (a) What was the purpose of the totem pole ?
   (b) What was the " Happy Hunting Ground " ?

9. What cruel forms of torture did the Red Indians inflict on their victims ?

10. Name two famous hunters who took part in many expeditions against Indians on the warpath.

DEVELOPMENT EXERCISES.

1. (a) Trace the " Termagant's " outward voyage on the map.
   (b) Trace the usual present-day shipping route between Liverpool and San Francisco.

2. The Red Indians were the original natives of North America. Who were the original natives of (a) Australia, (b) New Zealand, (c) South Africa ?

3. The crew ran short of provisions and rationing was introduced. What is the purpose of rationing ?

4. The blue bird appeared to be the special sign of that particular tribe. Of what countries are the following creatures the national emblems ?—lion, eagle, bear, kangaroo, beaver, springbok, elephant, cock, dragon.

5. Complete the following table. No. 1 is done for you:—

　　　　Father — Mother —- Son.
　　　　Man 　— Woman — ....
　　　　Brave 　— Squaw 　— ....
　　　　Negro — Negress — ....
　　　　King 　— Queen 　— ....

6. Maize is popularly known as " Indian " Corn. What national names are used for a special kind of the following ?—
.........Stew, 　　.........Rarebit, 　.........Bun,
.........Cakes, 　.........Sausage, 　.........Toffee,
.........Delight, 　.........Butter, 　.........Cheese,
.........Onions, 　.........Tart.

7. The Red Indians had different kinds of homes such as the tepee, wigwam, long house, and pueblo. Who live in the following ?—igloo, kraal, dowar, tent, caravan, manse, monastery, convent.

8. From the picture words on page 53 can you write the following sentences in the Indian language ?

　(a) Although it was a stormy morning the man killed a bear in the mountains.

　(b) At night, when the weather cleared, they had plenty of food in the Indian camp.

THE STORY OF PELORUS JACK

(Dolphins are sea-mammals which live in water and closely resemble fish in appearance. They belong to the same family as the whale and the porpoise, and, when fully grown, measure from eight to twelve feet long. Like the whales and porpoises, they enjoy the company of their own kind and are usually found in " schools.")

PERHAPS one of the strangest tales from " Down Under " is the story of a dolphin who made himself the pilot of certain ships, which voyaged through the channel between the North Island and South Island of New Zealand. If you were to hear the story from the native Maoris, or yarn-spinning sailors, you would at once think that it was far-fetched or pure invention, and that no such creature ever lived, but actually, most of the story would be quite true.

The coast of the South Island of New Zealand is dotted with numerous rocky islands and reefs having narrow channels with swift-flowing treacherous currents. This makes a voyage in these parts extremely dangerous, especially for any vessel unfamiliar with the safe and proper course. Consult the map on the opposite page, and you will see that the stretch of water between D'Urville Island and South Island is named French Pass,

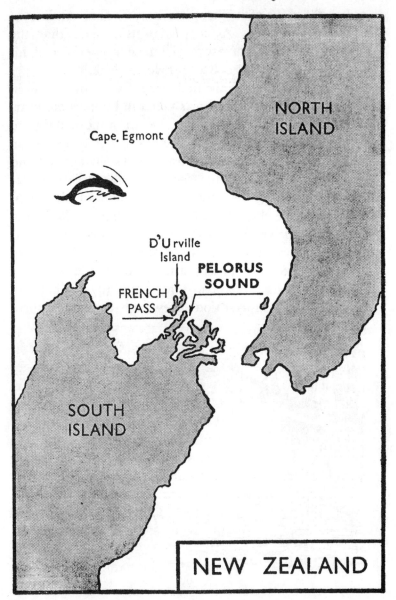

NORTH
ISLAND

Cape. Egmont

D'Urville
Island

**PELORUS
SOUND**

FRENCH
PASS

SOUTH
ISLAND

NEW ZEALAND

and to the right of it, there is a narrow channel, known as Pelorus Sound. As it was in this strait that the wonderful fish-like creature of our story performed his good deeds, he was called " Pelorus Jack."

When Jack made his first recorded appearance in 1871, only casual interest was taken in him. Some years later, when coastal steamers began almost daily to thread their way through French Pass, a purser on board one of these regular trading vessels, noticed and remarked on the strange fact that the creature was actually guiding the ship through one of the most dangerous stretches of water in that region. Jack kept in front of the vessel, and chose a safe course, well clear of the shallows and the many hidden reefs. The officer drew the attention of captains of other ships to the creature's regular habits, and gradually a halo of romance and superstition grew up around Pelorus Jack.

Day and night, year in year out, Jack was at his post, and, as you may imagine, the sailors discussed with great interest the actions of their strange friend. Some seamen, curious to know how long he had been performing this duty, questioned the Maoris. The natives stated that Pelorus Jack had been guiding their own large canoes for a long, long time. One old tribal chief recounted many stories in support of this, and declared that Jack had been known to his people, even in his father's youth. From his accounts too, it appeared that Jack and many of his kind had made their home in this channel, but they had all gradually disappeared until only he was left. Naturally, these answers puzzled the sailors more than ever, so they decided to keep a careful watch on their self-appointed guide, and this was what they discovered.

Pelorus Jack was shy of new steamers, and showed himself with freedom only to familiar ships, and he completely ignored sailing vessels. This latter point is peculiar, as fishes and sea-mammals approach ships under sail, with much more confidence than they would steamers. (The reason is that the creatures are scared by the noise and sight of the threshing propellers). When a ship came near to Jack's route, every passenger and every available member of the crew would eagerly scan the water, waiting for him to appear, as he had become almost as much of a mark as a lighthouse.

Suddenly, from some unknown hiding place, would appear a white streak in the blue sea, and, gambolling and leaping with every suggestion of joy, Jack would flash up to the bow of the ship, swerve and shoot ahead

—his pilot-work had begun. For several miles he would lead the vessel safely on its course, until he reached the open waters of French Pass. Here his duty ended and Jack returned to his home to await another steamer, so that he could guide her through the same perilous channel.

Passengers were fascinated by their strange escort, and many of them made special trips just to see him. Pelorus Jack soon became the chief topic of conversation among seafaring men, and his unique performance gave rise to much argument and debate. One suggestion was that he followed the vessels in order to obtain any food which might be thrown to him. Against this, however, eye-witnesses declared that he did not stop or feed while undertaking his self-imposed task.

The most puzzling question of all, and the one which led to the greatest disputes, was, " What kind of creature is Pelorus Jack ? " Some said he was a shark, some stated that he looked more like a large dugong (a sea-mammal which is supposed to be the origin of mermaid stories), while others maintained that he was a dolphin. Several snapshots were obtained and after careful examination it was finally decided that Pelorus Jack was a dolphin—a special type of dolphin known as a Risso Dolphin. Here is a description by one who had seen and photographed him at close quarters :—

" His colour is bluish-white, tinged with purple and yellow, and he has many irregular scars and scratches running in all directions. From his size and appearance, I am certain that Pelorus Jack is a dolphin."

Further proof was that dolphins feed on shell-fish and

cuttle-fish and the marks on Jack's skin were said to be caused by the suckers of the cuttle-fish.

It was not surprising that sailors and passengers on this route had a great affection for their pilot friend, and took great pride in his helpful friendliness. Nobody fully realised how much Jack was liked, until one day something happened, which nearly cost him his life.

Early one morning a vessel was about to enter Pelorus Sound, and, as usual, the deck of the ship was lined with people awaiting the appearance of the now famous dolphin. Sure enough, he appeared as if by magic, and the passengers shouted with delight as Jack made his usual inspection, and then dashed off in front to act as guide. Suddenly, while the engrossed spectators were watching every movement he made, a pistol shot rang out, and it was seen that Jack had been seriously hit. Consternation and anger seized the onlookers when they saw him flash away and disappear. The foolish culprit was told, in no uncertain terms, what the rest of the passengers thought of his treacherous deed, and, for the rest of the voyage, he was deservedly " sent to Coventry."

There was a very strange sequel to this shooting incident. It was said that Pelorus Jack had been shot at from the deck of the steamship " Penguin," and that he never again met or guided this ship. Many seamen refused to sail in the vessel because of the dolphin's behaviour and, peculiar to relate, the steamer was wrecked during a storm in Cook's Strait in 1909.

The cowardly act of firing at Jack did not deter other stupid and brutal tourists from trying to shoot him, and so, to safeguard his life from similar attempts, a special law was passed by the Government of New Zealand. This Order in Council " protected Pelorus Jack and all his genus in the waters of Cook's Strait, or in the bays, sounds, and estuaries adjacent thereto." An offence against this order was punishable by a fine of £100.

Jack's career, however, was not without further accident, as his friends could not guard him against the thousand and one risks of sea-life. On one occasion he was struck by the bow of a steamer, and this caused him to be absent from his beat. Month after month passed with no sign of the famous dolphin, and his disappearance caused some anxiety among his many friends. Then, when everyone had given up hope of ever seeing him again, there came, one day, an excited yell from the look-out of a passing ship.

" Pelorus Jack! " he shouted. " Pelorus Jack is back! "

The cry was quickly taken up, and the passengers rushed to the deck-rail to view and welcome their favourite. There was Jack dashing towards them at full speed, leaving a foamy wake behind him, and ready and eager to resume his friendly mission. Needless to say, everyone was delighted at his re-appearance and the good news spread like wildfire. The utmost care was taken to prevent further injury to this gallant and helpful creature, and he continued to guide ships in the sound as was his custom.

In 1912 Jack was again missed, and when the body of a dolphin was discovered on a beach in Cook's Strait, it was found to be none other than the mariner's guide and friend. Apparently he had been struck and fatally injured by the blade of a ship's propeller. The maritime world was grieved at the death of its mascot and mourned the loss of a true friend. It is a pity that Pelorus Jack was not preserved in a museum, as there could hardly be any creature of greater interest in natural history than the dolphin who performed so many good deeds and was specially protected by law.

(Adapted.)

QUESTIONS ON THE STORY.

1. What kind of creature is a dolphin ?
2. Name two other members of the same family.
3. Near which country did the story take place ?
4. Who were the natives of this country ?
5. Why was the creature called Pelorus Jack ?
6. When did he make his first recorded appearance ?
7. How did he introduce himself before beginning his pilot work ?
8. What did Pelorus Jack do when he reached the end of the dangerous channel ?
9. What excuse did some people make for his interest in passing vessels ?
10. Which kind of ships did Pelorus Jack completely ignore ?
11. Why was this peculiar ?
12. What question led to much argument among seafaring men ?
13. How was it proved that Pelorus Jack was a dolphin ?
14. What did a foolish passenger of a passing vessel try to do ?
15. How did the rest of the passengers show their disapproval ?
16. What was done to safeguard the life of Pelorus Jack ?
17. What injury caused him to be absent from his beat for several months ?
18. In what year did he die ?
19. What mishap caused his death ?
20. Where was his body found ?

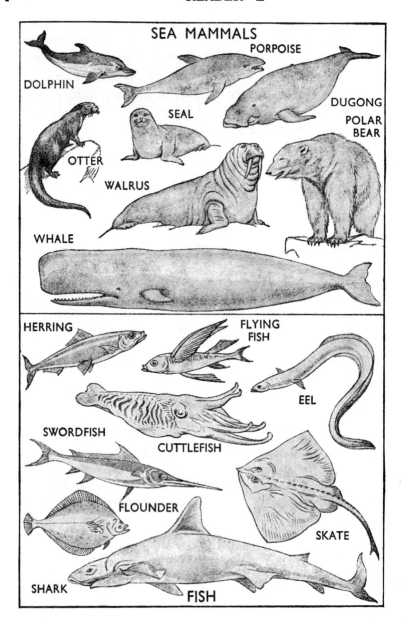

SEA MAMMALS

DOLPHIN

PORPOISE

SEAL

DUGONG

POLAR BEAR

OTTER

WALRUS

WHALE

HERRING

FLYING FISH

EEL

SWORDFISH

CUTTLEFISH

FLOUNDER

SKATE

SHARK

FISH

THE LEGEND OF THE WILLOW PATTERN.

ABOUT two hundred years ago, several Dutch merchants, who had been trading in the Far East, brought home some very peculiar and attractive pieces of porcelain from a little-known land called China. Among their many remarkable specimens were tiny bluish-white tea-sets with a quaint design of landscape and figures. These picture dishes were so much admired and sought after, that they soon became fashionable in many countries of Europe. Prominent in this favourite Chinese design was a willow tree, and the "Willow Pattern," as it was called, was faithfully copied by master craftsmen, and in a very short time the hardware shops contained wonderful imitations.

Now this strange Chinese picture on cup, saucer, and plate has a definite meaning, and is not merely a jumble of views to be seen in that strange land of the Orient, where so many habits and customs are altogether different from our own. In fact, it illustrates the story of a sad love romance, and, as this made a great appeal to many people, this special design became the most popular of the various picture dishes.

The picture of the plate on the following page shows

in detail the exact design as brought to Europe by those pioneer traders of the Netherlands. Notice on the right-hand side the palatial home of a wealthy lord or Mandarin. In the huge garden surrounding the house are seen a mulberry tree and an orange tree, both bearing abundant fruit. The rich man's estate is enclosed by a zig-zag bamboo fence, and nearby is an arched bridge showing three figures in the act of crossing. Immediately above is the "mournful, weeping willow tree," from which the name of this particular pattern was taken. To the left of this tree is a Chinese boat or sampan with a solitary figure in the stern. Beside it is a small island which contains a house not nearly as grand as the home of the rich noble. At the top can be seen two turtle doves in flight, both apparently attempting to entwine beaks. The following Chinese legend is said to be the story connecting all these figures.

Long, long ago, when the moon was still young, there lived in the land of Cathay a rich Mandarin who had an only daughter named Li-Chi. This maiden possessed great grace and charm, and was said to be more beautiful than all the stars of heaven. Her proud and selfish father intended that she should marry a wealthy nobleman of his own selection called Wang-Loo. Now Li-Chi could not bear the thought of marrying her parent's choice, as she knew him to be old, ugly and very bad-tempered. She refused to agree to the wedding and protested so strongly that her father flew into a terrible rage. When he saw that she was determined to have nothing to do with Wang-Loo, the father ordered his daughter to be kept a prisoner at his country palace until she would consent to marry the man whom he had chosen to be her husband.

For several weeks Li-Chi remained a prisoner in her father's beautiful country home, where she had everything she desired, except freedom to travel about and do as she pleased. Everybody admired the Mandarin's magnificent palace, which was said to contain some of the most valuable relics and ornaments in China. It was situated in the middle of a lovely garden, which was surrounded by a high bamboo fence barring admission to prying and unwelcome visitors. Of course, such a huge estate needed a great deal of care and attention, and to keep the place in perfect order, the Mandarin had engaged a large staff of servants.

It so happened that among the servants employed by her father was a young gardener named Chang. He was tall and handsome, and had long, almond-shaped eyes, light shining skin, and a slender pleated pig-tail. The Mandarin, snobbish and proud of his exalted station, spoke to him but little, and knew of him only as an honest and diligent workman. Chang, too, was proud, but his pride was in the garden, which he tended carefully and well.

One day, while the young man was hard at work, Li-Chi peeped through the bamboo lattice of her window and watched him examining the various blossoms. Admiring his handsome appearance and his skill with plants and flowers, she straightway fell in love with him. Chang, unaware that his master's beautiful daughter was spying upon him, crossed the garden and began to prune several rose-bushes, which grew beneath her window. When Li-Chi thought he was directly below, she looked out and slyly dropped a choice sweetmeat at his feet. Chang, who was bending at the time, saw the object fall at his feet and, on looking up quickly, caught a glimpse of the young lady as she withdrew her head. The gardener looked to see what had fallen from the window, and when he saw the surprise gift he was astonished. After picking up the unusual present, he selected and cut off the finest rose on the bushes, climbed the lattice, and stuck the flower through the slats. No sooner had he done so than he regretted his hasty action, for he knew that if the Mandarin should hear of it, he would be severely punished.

Later that night, when he visited his mother, who stayed on a neighbouring island, Chang told her of his adventure and bewailed his ill-fortune because, as a humble gardener, he could never hope to marry the lordly Mandarin's beautiful daughter. But the mother, who was a clever and capable woman, consoled her son and told him to pluck up courage as " Faint heart never won fair lady." She advised him not to despair, for despite his lack of worldly position and wealth, he still had a chance to win the charming Li-Chi as his bride.

Now Chang's mother reared silk-worms on her little island home and span silk for the Mandarin's household. On the following day she carried her usual weekly order of silk to Li-Chi and, during the course of conversation, the old lady revealed that her son secretly worshipped her. The Mandarin's daughter confessed that she was in love with Chang, but said that she could not see how they could ever be married, as her father would certainly rage and storm if he heard that she had lost her heart to one of such humble birth.

In time, a plan was arranged whereby Li-Chi was, on a certain night, to elope with her lover and steal away to a distant part of the country, where the young couple would be safe from the vengeance of her father. Everything was settled down to the smallest detail—Li-Chi was to be close by the rose-bushes in the garden at an appointed time, and Chang was to take her to his mother's home on the island where none would ever dream of looking for them. The mother advised Li-Chi to collect as much as she could of her valuables and jewellery so that, when she was reported missing, the Mandarin would believe that one of the many robbers who infested the adjoining country had stolen the jewels and abducted his daughter.

There is a proverb which states, " There's many a slip 'twixt cup and lip." The plan was so far carried out that the lovers succeeded in escaping unseen through the garden to the bridge, bearing between them, suspended on a stout bamboo pole, a large casket containing trinkets of gold and costly jewels. But it so happened that, just as they approached the bridge at the other end of which Chang's mother awaited them, the illustrious Mandarin chose to view his garden and, to his horror, beheld his only daughter running away with the low-born gardener.

Almost choking with anger, the father called on them to return, but they paid no heed to his cries. Seizing a long whip, the Mandarin rushed after them and, overtaking them while crossing the bridge, he grasped the luckless Chang by the pig-tail, twisted it round his neck, and beat him with a staff until he was senseless. Not content with this punishment the raging father hurled the unconscious gardener into the river where he sank and disappeared from view.

Meanwhile, poor Li-Chi, witnessing her lover's cruel fate, wrung her hands in grief. So great was her sorrow that, after scolding her father for his terrible deed, she suddenly sprang into the water, and she too vanished from sight. The proud Mandarin was stricken with remorse at the double tragedy, and never really recovered his health after the loss of his only daughter. Strange to relate, no trace of the lovers was ever found ; but at the side of the bridge, a beautiful willow tree sprang up and continually sighed a mournful dirge for the departed couple. Some time later, a pair of turtle-doves made their appearance and built a nest among its branches. There they would bill and coo the live-long day, secure from any interference.

Naturally, the people of the district connected the doves with the lovers, and so in the legend it is stated that the souls of the unfortunate couple took the shape of doves, and thus found the happiness they had longed for but lost.

(Adapted.)

INTERESTING FACTS
ABOUT
CHINA AND THE CHINESE.

1. In China, old people are thought to be wise and are always treated kindly by the young folk. There has been no lesson more widely taught than respect for parents, and this has gradually developed into the worship of ancestors. **Cathay** is the name given to China by the early writers.

2. The people have a dark-yellow or olive complexion, and it is noticeable that everyone has jet-black hair. Having a beard is an indication of age and dignity, and a man does not grow one until he is forty years old. Men wear loose blouses or coats and wide trousers tied at the ankles. Many women wear the same kind of clothes as the men, but quite a number have adopted the Western style of dress. The shoes are of cloth with thick felt soles.

3. **Rice** is the chief food of the people. The Chinese use bowls instead of plates, and **chopsticks** in place of knives and forks. **Pork** is also a popular food, while shark-fin soup and a soup made from a certain kind of bird-nest are regarded as very special dishes. Eating is an important event with the Chinese, and instead of greeting each other with " How do you do ? " or " Good day ! " they say " Have you eaten ? " It is rude to talk at meals as this means that you are neglecting the food provided by your host.

4. Many customs and habits appear to be the opposite of those in this country :—

(a) In Chinese names, the surname comes first, *e.g.* Fu Wong is Mr. Fu, **not** Mr. Wong.

(b) White is the mourning colour. At a funeral, a band playing noisy tunes leads the procession to the burial-ground. The loud blaring sound is said to drive away the evil spirits.

(c) It is polite for a host, wearing a Chinese skull-cap, to keep it on when receiving a guest. The host always uses both hands when giving anything to his guest. This shows that he gives ungrudgingly.

(d) Books begin where ours end—starting at the right-hand side of the page and reading upwards or downwards instead of across.

(e) When sewing, the Chinese woman inserts the needle in the cloth and pushes the needle away from her.

5. China has the greatest population of any single country in the world. In some parts, the housing problem is very serious and many people make their homes in house-boats and **sampans**. The rivers overflow their banks each year and the country suffers

dreadfully from **floods,** which destroy houses and crops and cause famine and disease.

6. Love of nature, politeness, and industrious habits are marks of this great people. Chinese of all ages are fond of **fireworks** and, at New Year time, all business stops, and they enjoy their holidays by setting off crackers and squibs. Young and old delight in the pastime of **kite-flying.** The "**Double Tenth**" (the tenth day of the tenth month—October) is celebrated as the anniversary of the Chinese Republic.

7. Some years ago, the binding of children's feet and the wearing of pig-tails were banned. A Chinese woman was considered beautiful if her feet were extremely small. With men, long finger-nails were a sign of wealth, as this showed that they did not need to work for a living. The unskilled workers are called **coolies.**

8. Along the Chinese coast may be seen the peculiar-looking sailing ships known as **Junks.** In certain parts of the country they have a quaint form of fishing. Sea-birds called **cormorants** are tamed and their long necks are ringed to prevent them from swallowing the fish which they catch for their masters.

9. The Chinese invented **paper** and were the sole

makers of it for over seven centuries. They also knew how to **print** and how to make **gunpowder** long before other nations. The Chinese discovered how to turn a mixture of clay and sand into **porcelain**, and they have never been equalled in the making and decorating of beautiful dishes.

10. **The Great Wall of China**, which was built to keep enemies from invading the country, is the greatest barrier ever constructed by the hands of man. It is about 1,500 miles long, and extends the whole length of the northern border from the sea to Tibet. The wall is the height of a two-storey building and is as wide as a country road on top. At certain points there are turrets for defence and gateways for road traffic.

QUESTIONS ON THE STORY.

1. Who first brought Chinese picture dishes to Europe ?
2. What was the most popular design called ?
3. In what colour was it painted ?
4. Name as many things in the picture as you can remember.
5. Give another name for China.
6. Whom did the rich Mandarin order his daughter to marry ?
7. Why did Li-Chi refuse ?
8. How did her father punish her for disobeying him ?
9. Describe Chang's appearance.
10. What gift did Li-Chi throw to the young gardener ?
11. What did Chang do when he received the present ?
12. Where did the young gardener's mother stay ?
13. What was her occupation ?
14. With what proverb did she encourage her son ?
15. Where did Li-Chi meet Chang by arrangement ?
16. Why did she take her valuables and jewellery with her ?
17. How were their plans upset ?
18. What did the Mandarin take with him to punish them ?
19. What happened to the young couple ?
20. What appeared at the same spot some time later ?

QUESTIONS ON THE INTERESTING FACTS.

1. (a) What good lesson has been widely taught in China ?
   (b) Into what has this developed ?
   (c) What did early writers call China ?
2. Describe Chinese dress and appearance.
3. (a) What is the chief food of the people ?
   (b) What do they use in place of knives and forks ?
   (c) Describe a special Chinese dish.
4. Describe two customs or habits that appear to be the opposite of those in this country.
5. What cause dreadful famine and disease each year ?
6. Name a very popular pastime.
7. (a) What cruel custom has now been banned ?
   (b) What is the name given to a general unskilled labourer ?

8. Describe a peculiar form of fishing to be seen in China.
9. Name two important Chinese inventions or discoveries.
10. Describe the Great Wall of China.

DEVELOPMENT EXERCISES.

1. Point out China on the map. Of what continent is it a part ?
   Look again at the map and explain why it is said to be in
   the Far East. Name another country in the same region.

2. This story is entitled " The Legend of the Willow Pattern."
   What is a (a) legend, (b) folk-tale, (c) fairy-tale, (d) myth,
   (e) parable ?

3. China is sometimes called " The Land of the Plum Blossom."
   What countries are often referred to as (a) The Land of the
   Thistle, (b) The Land of the Rose, (c) The Land of the
   Daffodil, (d) The Land of the Shamrock, (e) The Land of the
   Maple Leaf, (f) The Land of the Tulip ?

4. The Chinese, in conversation, often quote clever sayings of
   Confucius, a wise man of ancient times. Give half a dozen
   well-known English proverbs.

5. From a name, we can sometimes tell to what country a person
   belongs, e.g. Fu Wong—China. Of what countries are the
   following likely to be natives :—Evan Jones, Ali Mohammed,
   Iain MacDonald, Hiram K. Hickes, Patrick O'Connor ?

6. The Chinese are very fond of fireworks. What special name is
   given to the day on which we hold an annual display of crackers
   and squibs ? Give exact date.

7. You would buy Willow Pattern dishes in a hardware shop.
   In what kinds of shops would you buy (a) flowers, (b) stockings,
   (c) hats, (d) vegetables ?

8. Chinese boys and girls are noted for their good manners.
   How can boys and girls show their good manners in
   (a) the home, (b) the school, (c) the street ?

AULD LANG SYNE.

Should Auld acquaintance be forgot
    and never brought to mind,
Should auld acquaintance be forgot
    and days of Auld Lang Syne,
For Auld Lang Syne my dear,
For Auld Lang Syne,
We'll tak' a cup o' kindness yet,
    for Auld Lang Syne.

LINSTEAD MARKET

1. Carry me ackie go a Linstead Market
   Not a quattie would sell
   Carry me ackie go a Linstead Market
   Not a quattie would sell

   Refrain.

   Lord, not a mite, not a bite,
   What a Saturday night
   Lord, not a mite, not a bite,
   What a Saturday night.

LONDONDERRY AIR. *(Oh! Erin Dear).*

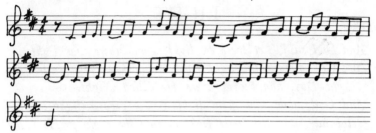

Oh! Erin dear, my thoughts are with thee ever
No other land can stir my heart like thee
Why did I from my friends and dear ones sever
To make my home so far across the sea?
I miss thy jovial sons and winsome daughters
The songs of children on the village green,
I yearn to hear the sound of rushing waters
And more than all I miss my faithful sweet Eileen.

ALL THROUGH THE NIGHT. *(Ar Hyd y Nos.)*

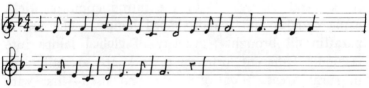

Sleep my love and peace attend thee,
    All through the night;
Guardian angels God will lend thee,
    All through the night;
Soft the drowsy hours are creeping,
Hill and dale in slumber steeping,
Love alone his watch is keeping —
    All through the night.

LIGHT

And God said, Let there be light : and there was light.
And God divided the light from the darkness and called the
light Day, and the darkness He called Night.
And God made two great lights ; the greater light to rule
the day, and the lesser light to rule the night : He made
the stars also.

GENESIS, Chapter 1.

IN earliest times man discovered that by rubbing
stones together sparks could be given off to set
dried wood alight. The sticks burned and thus the
ordinary **faggot fire** became the first man-made lamp
and stove. When only light was needed a **kindling
stick** or **firebrand** containing pitch was set ablaze.

The first shaped lamps were **stone bowls** containing
tallow but they were not successful as they were very
smoky and smelly. With the introduction of **wicks**
came **candles** and **teapot-shaped lamps**. The use of
paraffin oil brought a variety of **globed lamps** into
fashion. Different forms of these lamps are still used
in rural areas. **Coal gas** was next used—first with
metal burners, which gave a fan-shaped flame—
then with **mantles** and **globes**. The discovery of
electricity changed all that had gone before and
completely overcame the disadvantages of tallow, pitch,
oil, and gas. It may be seen in a variety of forms—
ordinary pear-shaped bulbs, battery torches, lighting in
long glass tubes, and searchlights.

THE NERVOUS LAWYER

A FRENCH lawyer had been hastily summoned to the bedside of an old friend in order to draw up his last will and testament. After a three-mile journey, the lawyer, a very nervous and excitable man, arrived just in time ; the will was duly signed, and a little later the patient passed away.

Meanwhile the lawyer sat cowering over the fire, aghast at the scene that was passing before him, and striving now and then to keep up his false courage by a glass of wine. Already his fears were on the alert and the idea of contagion flitted to and fro through his mind. In order to quiet these thoughts, he lighted his pipe and began to prepare for returning home. At that moment the doctor in attendance turned round to him and said :—

" Dreadful time, this ! The trouble seems to be spreading."

" What trouble ? " exclaimed the lawyer, with a movement of surprise.

" Two died yesterday and three to-day," continued the doctor without answering the question. " very serious epidemic, sir—very."

" But what trouble is it ? What disease has carried off my friend so suddenly ? "

" What disease? Why, scarlet fever, to be sure."

" And is it infectious? "

" Unfortunately, very much so."

" Then I am a dead man ! " exclaimed the agitated lawyer, putting his pipe into his waistcoat pocket, and beginning to walk up and down the room in despair. " I am a dead man ! Now, doctor, don't deceive me—don't, will you? What—what are the symptoms of scarlet fever? "

" High temperature and a sharp burning pain in the side," answered the doctor.

" Oh ! What a fool I was to come here ! " shouted the now trembling lawyer.

In vain did the housekeeper and the doctor strive to soothe and pacify him—he was not a man to be reasoned with ; he answered that he knew the state of his own health better than they did, and insisted upon going home without delay. That was easier said than done, as the carriage in which he had come had returned to the city. At this late hour it would be difficult to hire a vehicle of any description because the whole neighbourhood was abed and asleep. What was to be done? There was no other way out of the situation but to take the doctor's horse, which stood at the door patiently waiting for his master.

Well, as there was no other remedy, our lawyer mounted this raw-boned steed and set forth upon his homeward journey. The night was cold and gusty and the wind blew right in his teeth. Overhead, the leaden clouds were beaten to and fro, and through them the newly risen moon seemed to be tossing and drifting along like a tiny boat in the surf, now swallowed up in a huge billow of cloud, and again lifted upon its bosom and dashed with silvery spray. The trees by the roadside groaned with a sound of evil omen ; and before him lay three dreary miles, beset with a thousand imaginary perils. Obedient to the whip and spur, the steed leaped forward by fits and starts—now dashing away in a tremendous gallop, and now relaxing into a long, hard trot ; while the rider, filled with dread of the disease and fear of impending death, urged on the animal as if he were being pursued by the Evil Spirit himself.

In this way, by dint of whistling and shouting, and beating the horse right and left, one mile of the fatal three was safely passed. The scared lawyer had so far subsided that he suffered the poor animal to walk up-hill ; but suddenly his fears were revived with tenfold violence by a sharp pain in the right side, which seemed to pierce him like a needle.

" It is upon me at last ! " groaned the fear-stricken man. " Must I die in a ditch after all ? " Then he yelled to the horse, " Hi ! get up—get up ! "

Away went the horse and rider at full speed—hurry-scurry—up hill and down—panting and blowing like a whirlwind. At every leap the pain in the rider's side seemed to increase. At first it was a pin-point—then it spread to the size of a sixpence—then it covered a place as large as the palm of your hand. The disease was gaining upon him fast. The poor man groaned aloud in agony ; faster and faster sped the horse over the frozen ground—farther and farther spread the pain over his side. To complete the dismal picture, the storm commenced—snow mingled with rain. But snow and rain and cold were nought to him ; for, though his arms and legs were frozen to icicles, he felt it not ; the fatal symptom was upon him ; he knew that he was doomed to die—not of cold, but of scarlet fever!

At length, he knew not how, more dead than alive, he eventually reached the gates of the city. A band of stray dogs, that were howling at a street corner, seeing the lawyer dash by, joined in the hue and cry, and the mongrels ran barking and yelping at the animal's heels. It was now late at night, and only here and there a solitary lamp twinkled from an upper storey window. But on went the lawyer, up this street and down that, till at last he reached his own door. There was a light in his wife's bedroom. The good woman came to the window, alarmed at such a knocking and howling and clattering at her door so late at night.

" Let me in ! let me in ! Quick ! quick ! " he

exclaimed, almost breathless from terror and fatigue.

" Who are you, that come to disturb a lone woman at this hour of the night ? " cried a sharp voice from above. " Begone about your business at once, and let quiet people sleep."

" Oh, hurry, hurry! Come down and let me in! I am your husband. Don't you know my voice ? Quick, I beseech you—or I will die here in the street."

After a few moments of explanation and delay, the door was opened, and the lawyer stalked into his own house, pale and haggard in aspect, and as stiff and as straight as a ghost. Cased from head to foot in an armour of ice, as the glare of the lamp fell upon him he looked like a mailed knight of bygone days. But in one place his armour was broken. On his right side was a circular spot, as large as the crown of a hat, and about as black!

" My dear wife! " he exclaimed, with more tenderness than he had shown for years, " reach me a chair. My hours are numbered. I am a dying man! "

Alarmed at these exclamations, his wife quickly stripped off his overcoat. Something fell from beneath it, and was dashed to pieces on the hearth. It was the lawyer's pipe! He placed his hand upon his side, and lo! it was bare to the skin! Coat, waistcoat and linen were burnt through and through, and there was a huge blister on his side.

The mystery was soon explained, symptom and all. The lawyer, in his excitement, had put his pipe into his pocket without knocking out the red hot ashes.

Adapted from "Outre-Mer," by H. W. Longfellow.

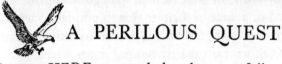

A PERILOUS QUEST

" WHERE on earth has he gone ? "

There was a note of impatience, almost of annoyance, in Ian MacDonald's voice, the sort of vexation one is apt to feel when one has been searching for a person for several hours without success, but aware all the time that he can't be very far away.

" He " was Neil MacKenzie ; and for the last three weeks, hardly an hour had passed during which Ian and Neil had not been together. When Ian had come down to breakfast that morning, having noticed that the second bed in the little room was vacant, his first question had been : " Where is Neil ? " But neither Duncan MacKenzie nor his wife could tell him any more than that Neil must have risen very early and gone out. Early risers themselves, they had seen nothing of their son that morning.

So, breakfast eaten, Ian had taken his gun and gone off for a ramble on his own; a ramble that led to the likeliest places where his friend might be. But no sign of Neil had he happened upon. Vexing indeed ; for Ian's holiday was drawing near its end, and this promised to be the only suitable day for the sailing and fishing excursion on Loch Laggan that had been discussed the evening before.

Nine years back, when only seven years of age, Ian had left the Highlands. An unexpected legacy had come to his father, and in deference to the wishes of his wife, Donald MacDonald had left his small estate in the care of Duncan MacKenzie and gone south.

This was Ian's first return to his birthplace, where he had been only too glad to renew his friendship with Neil, now a short but sturdy young man three years older than himself. Hearty indeed had been the welcome to " the young laird," as the MacKenzie family persisted in calling Ian, and each of them vied with the other to make him comfortable and keep him agreeably occupied. True Highlander, Ian was grieved beyond words that in a few days' time he must turn his back on the land of his clan, and return to occupations much less pleasing than shooting and fishing, tramping the wild moors, and climbing the heathery hillsides.

Several hours had gone by and Ian was thinking of turning back. He was growing hungry, and the close proximity of Creag Ard, or the High Rock, a steep cliff crowned with a pile of jumbled rocks and over-looking a tiny tarn, warned him that he was already six miles from the farm. All at once, his attention was caught and held by the sight of a couple of dark specks in movement high up across the pearl-gray sky. At once the idea of immediate return left him. Those specks were eagles.

The Highlands still hold specimens of that glorious bird, the golden eagle, but during his holiday Ian had not been lucky enough to get so much as a glimpse of one. The present chance was too good to be missed.

Watching, he saw the twin specks swiftly grow larger as the birds dropped, making more than one spiral turn as they descended. Nearing the earth, their speed became tremendous. It was clear they had viewed a likely quarry and were swooping down on it. Forgetting his hunger, forgetting Neil, Ian let out a whoop and started to run quickly towards the High Rock, some part of which was obviously the birds' objective. The sight of an eagle actually taking its prey was something that Ian had never witnessed. It would be a sight never to be forgotten.

But the interest the lad felt became tense and gripping excitement, and his pace increased as he came in sight of a small level stretch of rock some thirty feet below the actual crest of the peak. Above the patch hovered the two eagles ; on it was their quarry ; and a thrill of horror ran through Ian. On his knees was a man, head bound with a rag, his arms raised in feeble defence against the persistent attacks from the long, taloned claws striking at him. The man was Neil.

Rising a few yards, falling, ever on the move, hackles of their curved necks bristling, incessantly fluttering their mighty wings, the birds assailed their victim with fury, uttering the while savage cries that sounded like " Kooluk ! Klook ! "

The courage of the golden eagle, when hungry, is such that it will not hesitate to attack a fully grown deer, if its anger be sufficiently aroused. Even man is not exempt, as the Highland shepherds and ghillies well know, and a man, unarmed and in such obvious plight as was Neil, would stand but a mighty poor

chance against the onslaught of powerful wing blows and the steel-like three-inch talons of two such assailants.

Yelling as he ran, Ian swung the gun from his shoulder, grasping the barrel with both hands. The eagles became aware of him, and, as he neared his kneeling, swaying friend, the smaller of the pair suddenly swerved in its swoop, planed off in a slanting flight, and winged its way upwards. But the other, an immense fellow, with a spread of wing that to Ian appeared to be almost the width of the farm-house kitchen, was either hungrier or more angry. At once it made evident that the sight of Ian was not sufficient to cause it to be willing to give up its prey. Attack was speedily transferred to the active enemy.

As Ian checked on reaching Neil, the big eagle swept upon him with a circling movement ; and as the lad swung the butt of his gun at the thrust-forward head, with its wicked-looking hooked bill and angrily burning eyes of clear orange brown, he received a clout from a wing that hurled him aside, and sent him spinning as though some huge hand had dealt him a violent box on the ear. His own well-intended blow went astray, and Ian found himself in painful contact with the rock.

Ears singing, he scrambled to his feet, not a great deal hurt, but in a passion of anger. And he was only just in time. From some ten feet above his head, the bird was nearing him in a second swoop, screaming its "Kooluk! Klook!" more vehemently than before. He ducked and dodged aside, striking upward a blow that missed by many inches. Then he was compelled to whirl about; for through the tail of his eye he noticed that the cunning enemy, suddenly checking, was swerving towards him from behind. He ducked, dropping to one knee as he jabbed upward. He felt the impact with the brown and red tinted body, but it was too slight to assure him he had done the bird any serious injury.

In spite of what he had heard—from Duncan MacKenzie and others—that the eagle seldom uses its bill for other purposes than the tearing to pieces of the flesh upon which it feeds, Ian was a good deal more nervous of the hooked black and yellow beak than of the creature's claws. It was at the head he aimed most of his blows—a small and ever-moving target not at all easy to hit.

Moreover, he found himself becoming bewildered, his sight confused, by the amazing speed of his enemy, and the continual changes of the angles of attack. Again and again he struck, for the butt to meet nothing more solid than air. But his nerve did not desert him. Fear was wiped out by rage, and by the intense desire to get his own back on this formidable foe.

Then disaster befell him. In avoiding a fierce stroke from the enormous claws, Ian overbalanced. He stumbled ; a wing smote the back of his head, and for the second time he was bowled over. As he met the ground, he felt the gun snap where the barrel joins the lock.

Dismayed, he sprang upright, looking wildly around. Not a yard away was Neil, still on his knees, making a vain effort to get up, but too dazed to lend the slightest assistance. But the same glance showed him something else—a small-bladed axe lying near Neil. In an instant Ian's fingers were gripping the handle of the axe. Again he faced the eagle. Too much was being asked of him at the moment for anything to be possible ; he acted by instinct. Now, as the bird drove at him, instead of trying to evade the attack by leaping aside, he nerved himself to stand fast. Left arm flung across his face to guard his eyes from the steel-tipped claws, he poised the axe ready for a decisive blow. To deal such a blow, his stroke must be delayed until he was within range of the fearsome talons.

Ian had not long to wait. As it was, the temptation to close his eyes was difficult to overcome. But a change in the bird's tactics helped him. Instead of trying a direct swoop at the head, the eagle began to move in circles, just outside striking distance, and Ian was forced to activity so that he should continue to face the foe.

Suddenly the creature darted towards him and struck. He had a glimpse of the underside of the open claws—a full seven inches across—and in desperation he slashed forward, the axe aimed six inches above the left claw, which was almost touching his guard arm as he launched the blow. He felt the edge of the axe meet something solid, but the blow, aimed at the malevolent, lurid eyes, went astray. Either a slight error of judgment or his arm had straightened too much, for it was among the gold-striped hackles behind the almost bare skull that the edge buried itself.

Panting, every nerve tingling, Ian stepped back a pace, ready to renew the battle, and heartened by the hoarse scream of pain to which the bird gave vent. But the fight was over. Two seconds later, after a hesitant fluttering to and fro, the eagle abruptly wheeled and shot away, rising higher and higher with every beat of its huge wings.

" Thank goodness ! " exclaimed Ian, in his native Gaelic, though not a word of the tongue had he spoken since leaving his Highland home as a child of seven. His knees suddenly went slack, and he sank rather than sat down.

It was only a temporary weakness, however. Almost immediately he pulled himself together and was kneeling beside his friend, who had fainted. A few minutes later, Neil had recovered sufficiently to be able, with Ian to support him, to reach the tarn below. A long drink of cold water, and bathing of the several ugly wounds a removal of the bandage revealed, still further revived him. Tearing off his own shirt sleeves, Ian made pads and bandages for the injuries and, after half an hour's rest, Neil declared himself able to walk back to the farm. But it was a long and painful journey, with many halts, and more than once Neil was glad of his companion's arm. It was almost time for the evening meal before the farm was reached.

On the way down, Neil told what had happened. Knowing where the eyrie was situated, he had gone to it. He had been leaning over the great nest when the female eagle had suddenly appeared and at once attacked him furiously. Unable to make much of a defence, blood streaming from his head, he had received a swipe from one of her wings that had sent him sprawling. How he got away from the place and down to a safer level he could not remember.

" But what were you doing at the nest ? " asked Ian curiously.

" There was one egg, and I wanted it for you," replied Neil simply. " Last night, as we talked, you said you would like an eagle's egg to give to a friend of yours in England, and I thought that I would go early so as to be able to give it to you at breakfast. And I did not get it ! Now she will never leave the nest again until the egg is hatched," he concluded dismally.

" Bother the egg ! cried Ian. " You're safe, Neil ; and that's all that matters."

From " Young England," by George Surrey.

INTERESTING FACTS
ABOUT
BIRDS OF PREY.

1. There are birds which pursue, kill, and devour smaller and weaker creatures, and there are others which search for dying animals and wait until their victims are lifeless before starting to feed upon them. These birds are flesh-eaters and are called **Birds of Prey**. They can be easily recognised by their strong, hooked beaks and powerful talons.

2. The king of birds of prey is the **Eagle**, which lives largely on flesh and kills such creatures as birds, rabbits, hares, and even lambs. Usually the eagle catches its prey by swooping down on its victim and carrying it off in its great strong talons. The nest, called an **eyrie**, is situated in some high cliff or mountain, where there is little chance of the **eaglets** being disturbed.

3. The chief enemy of small birds is the **Falcon**. His usual method of attack is to pursue his quarry on the wing, strike with his cruel talons, and pick up the lifeless victim from the ground. In early times these birds were trained to hunt and kill game. The **peregrine falcon** is considered the swiftest bird in the British Isles and it can overtake an express train travelling at full speed.

4. The **Hawk** family, consisting of **goshawk, sparrow-hawk, merlin-hawk,** and the **kestrel,** destroy large numbers of our small birds and do much mischief among chickens. Hawks hunt in the same manner as falcons and though they are fierce birds, they are very light and graceful in their movements.

5. The **Owl,** owing to his grave and solemn look, is said to be the symbol of wisdom. He is an enemy of small birds and, in the silence of the night, pounces on his victims. Strange to say, he lives mostly on rats and mice, and hunts only in the dark, as he cannot see well in daylight. Both of his large unblinking eyes look forwards, whereas in other birds the eyes look in different directions.

6. The villains among British birds are the members of the **Crow** tribe. The **hooded crow** is a nasty, sly creature and every young bird within reach is the victim of his cruel beak. Usually " hoodies " hunt in couples and they devour a huge number of the eggs of smaller birds. Because of its continual attacks on sick animals, lambs, and birds, farmers shoot the **Raven** on sight. This horrid creature is said to be a bird of ill-omen.

7. There are several kinds of **Vultures,** such as **Condors, Turkey-Vultures,** and **Black Vultures.** Although they are large birds, their claws are not strong enough to carry off their prey. They are lazy and cowardly, and seldom attack their victims while alive. These birds are said to have great powers of sight and flight in search of food, and in many eastern countries vultures are protected by law because they are useful as scavengers.

BIRDS OF PREY

PEREGRINE FALCON

SPARROW-HAWK

BUZZARD

GOLDEN EAGLE

VULTURE

ALBATROSS

CROW

OWL

RAVEN

8. The **Buzzard** is another fierce enemy of small birds and closely resembles the eagle in flight and habits. They are said to be found in most parts of the world.

9. The **Secretary Bird** of Africa is so called because of the long feathers that look like quills behind the ears. This bird resembles an eagle with very long legs, and although it has little power of flight, it can run very quickly over the ground.   No one is allowed to kill this bird, which is protected by law, as it destroys an enormous number of poisonous reptiles.

10. The giant of the sea-bird race is the **Albatross**, which is about the size of a full-grown turkey and has a wing span as high as a door.   This bird lives mostly at sea and only comes ashore at nesting times.   The albatross feeds on shell-fish, cuttle-fish, and carrion. Sailors say that to harm or kill this bird brings bad luck.

QUESTIONS ON THE STORY.

1. In what part of Scotland did the story take place ?
2. Give the full names of the two lads.
3. How old were they ?
4. How had Ian been spending his holidays ?
5. What title did the MacKenzie family persist in giving him ?
6. Why was Ian so vexed at his chum's disappearance ?
7. What did he take with him when he went in search of Neil ?
8. What was the name of the steep cliff ?
9. How far was it from the farm ?
10. What caught Ian's attention and aroused his curiosity ?
11. Why did a thrill of horror run through him ?
12. What happened to his gun during the early stages of the fight ?
13. With what other weapon did he continue the struggle ?
14. What two words resembled the eagle's scream ?

15. What were the bird's chief weapons of attack ?
16. Why did Neil take no part in the struggle ?
17. How did the fight end ?
18. What did Ian use to bind his companion's injuries ?
19. About what time did the lads arrive home after their exciting adventure ?
20. Why had Neil gone alone on such a dangerous expedition ?

QUESTIONS ON THE INTERESTING FACTS.

1. (a) What name is given to a flesh-eating bird ?
   (b) How can such birds be easily recognised ?
2. What bird is said to be the " King of Birds," and what name is given to its nest ?
3. What bird is considered the swiftest in the British Isles ? Describe the once popular sport in which it was used.
4. Name three members of the hawk family.
5. What bird is said to be the symbol of wisdom ? When does it hunt for food ? Why ?
6. Who are the villains among British birds ? Name two members of this tribe.
7. What is the difference between a vulture and an eagle ? How are vultures looked upon in some eastern countries ?
8. Which bird of prey is found in most parts of the world ?
9. What is peculiar about the Secretary Bird of Africa ? Why is it protected by law ?
10. What is the largest sea-bird ? What do superstitious sailors say about it ?

DEVELOPMENT EXERCISES.

1. In what country did the story take place ? Point it out on the map.
2. What language did the boys speak when they were very young ? Name other parts of the British Isles where the natives speak a language other than English.

3. Although not mentioned in the story, what special kind of dress might these boys have worn ? Is it commonly worn throughout Scotland ? How can you tell the clan to which a person so dressed belongs ?

4. The lads spent the holiday shooting and fishing, climbing the hills, and tramping the moors. Would you like this kind of holiday or would you prefer a holiday at a farming village, or a fishing village, or a popular seaside resort ? Give reasons for your answer.

5. Birds of prey have very good eye-sight. What do people wear when they have poor eye-sight ? What do we use to see things clearly at a great distance ? What instrument helps us to see things which we cannot see with the naked eye ?

6. Birds of prey are swift fliers. Name any birds which (*a*) seldom fly, (*b*) cannot fly.

7. The eagle is called " The King of Birds." Which creatures would you say were (*a*) The King of Animals, (*b*) The Tiger of the Ocean ? Do you know of any titles sometimes given to certain animals ?

8. (*a*) The eagle nests in high places where there is little danger of being disturbed. Can you name any birds which nest (1) in trees or bushes, (2) on the ground, (3) in the eaves of houses, (4) on the sides of cliffs ?

   (*b*) Do you approve of taking eggs from birds' nests ? Give reasons for your answer.

A BOASTER BEATEN

AWAY in the far and frozen north, amid the ice and snow of Greenland, there lived a sturdy little Eskimo boy named Katerparsuk. Unfortunately, he had lost both his father and mother, and the members of his tribe paid little attention to him. Knowing that he was dependent on his relatives, the lad tried to make himself as useful as possible, and so pay back what kindness was shown to him.

It was Katerparsuk's secret ambition to become the best and bravest hunter of the tribe. This was going to prove a struggle against great odds, for none of the men would bother to teach or help him in any way. Thus, while other boys of his own age were being taught by their parents how to hunt and slay the various animals to be found in that desolate region, the lonely boy was forced to loiter about the village, doing odd jobs of no real service to the tribe.

But Katerparsuk was not to be beaten and, by being observant and listening attentively to the hunters recounting their adventures, he picked up a great deal of valuable information about tracking, trapping, and killing such animals as the seal, walrus, and polar bear.

One day he decided to build himself a kayak, or skin-canoe, for, having a boat of his own, he could become more or less independent of the others. This, however, was easier said than done, and for a long time he was disheartened, because he could not obtain a skin with which to make his little craft. Then, when he least expected it, good fortune smiled on him.

While wandering along the sea-shore some distance from the village he found the body of a dead seal. Great was his joy and pulling out his crude home-made knife, he quickly set to work and stripped off the skin, which he then hung in a secret place. As soon as the boy had finished this task, he hastened to the village and, obtaining the loan of a sledge, returned to take home the carcase of the seal and share it among his tribesmen. In exchange for some of the meat, he was given several wooden spars, for which he had begged so often and which had always been refused.

When Katerparsuk had all he needed to build his craft, he immediately started to cut the shape and framework of his kayak. Once this was ready, the boy went to the spot where he had hidden the seal-skin and returned with it to complete his boat. First he soaked the skin in sea-water ; then he stretched it tightly over the framework and carefully sewed it in place, at the same time taking great pains to keep the skin as watertight as possible. No one offered to help him, and, as everything was done without assistance, Katerparsuk took great pride in his little kayak.

There was one lad, however, who did his utmost to hinder and annoy the orphan boy while at his work.

This big bully, Tutiak by name, was very unpopular with all the members of the tribe, as he was nothing more than a boaster and a coward. Quite often he tried to spoil Katerparsuk's kayak, but despite his unwelcome attentions, the boy carried on as best he could.

On the day that he was putting the finishing touches to the boat, the sly Tutiak dressed himself in a polar bear's skin and, with a loud grunt, rushed at the unsuspecting boy. Immediately Katerparsuk saw the supposed bear close beside him, he threw down his tools and, without once looking back, fled to the shelter of the nearest igloo. Later he discovered that it was Tutiak in disguise, and the big bully did his best to make him the laughing-stock of the village, by joking to everyone about the incident, mocking his fear, poking fun at his little boat, and behaving as only a coward can to one smaller and weaker than himself.

At last the kayak was made seaworthy and, having passed inspection by his elders, the boy was able to go out hunting every day that weather permitted. On quite a number of occasions Katerparsuk managed to kill a seal or a walrus, and his return was always eagerly awaited by the old people of the tribe, for, after taking his own small share, he would distribute the rest of his catch amongst them. Thus the once despised boy became a general favourite and was acclaimed a most promising hunter.

Years passed, and Katerparsuk grew to be an athletic young man, and was regarded as a brave and fearless slayer of wild animals. The only snag was that Tutiak persisted in relating the incident of the " bear " on every possible occasion, and thus branded him as lacking in courage. Naturally, this caused bitter rivalry between the two hunters, and each tried to out-do the other in feats of daring and skill.

On one very dangerous expedition, Katerparsuk killed a huge walrus, the largest ever caught by any member of the tribe, and while taking his prize home by sledge, he thought of a plan to pay back his old enemy Tutiak. On arrival at the village he skinned the walrus, soaked the pelt in sea-water, and left it to dry. Two days later the skin had become so hard and so stiff that, if it were struck by a harpoon, the weapon would merely glance off without doing any harm. The hunter then sewed the skin into the shape of a walrus, leaving an opening so that he could crawl inside it.

Katerparsuk waited until he knew his rival was out

hunting seal and walrus. The chief weapon used in this type of hunting was a harpoon to which there was attached a long line with an air-bladder at the end. If the harpoon was thrown and missed its intended victim, the air-bladder floated, thus indicating the position of the weapon and making its recovery much easier. If the harpoon was thrown and struck its objective, the air-bladder retarded the progress of the wounded creature trying to escape.

Katerparsuk, after seeing that no one was about, took out the walrus-skin and his fishing lines, and departed for the hunting grounds. When he noticed Tutiak entering the bay in which he had just started to fish, he quickly donned the walrus-skin, dived into the icy-cold water, and swam towards the kayak. The hunter saw what appeared to be a fine specimen of a walrus swimming out of the bay and he immediately gave chase. Once within striking distance, Tutiak hurled his harpoon at the walrus, and to his amaze-

ment saw his weapon hit the animal with a resounding whack and bounce harmlessly into the sea. What astonished him most of all was that the creature turned, grabbed his harpoon, line, and air-bladder, and made off as fast as it could swim.

It is considered a great disgrace for an Eskimo to lose his harpoon, and the hunter was at his wit's end as to how he could explain the loss of his weapon. On his way home he invented a story, and told his kinsfolk at the village that he had encountered a huge walrus, much bigger than that slain by Katerparsuk. After a fierce struggle (so he said), the monster had seized his harpoon and made off.

The natives listened to his tale with great interest, and at once he saw a fine opportunity to command their admiration. He added many graphic details to his account of the desperate fight, until his listeners began to think that only a hero could have escaped from such a terrible foe. Katerparsuk said nothing, but listened intently to every telling of the story by Tutiak, who was considered, as a result of this encounter, to be the most daring and courageous hunter of the tribe.

Several days later, Katerparsuk had the good fortune to slay half-a-dozen large seals, and, to celebrate the event, he invited the men of the village to a feast in his igloo. Naturally everyone accepted the invitation, as seal-meat is the favourite food of the Eskimo. Among those present was the braggart Tutiak, and it was not long until he began to re-tell the story of his terrible encounter with the gigantic walrus, and as usual, he added incidents to illustrate his own bravery. While the company listened to the oft-repeated story, Katerparsuk rose quietly, and, going over to a recess in the wall of the igloo, took out the walrus-skin, and the missing harpoon, line and air-bladder.

Returning to the circle of his guests, he stood facing Tutiak and said, " Here is your long-lost weapon : and, as you can easily see, your mark is upon the air-bladder. On the day of which you speak I disguised myself in this walrus-skin, and swam towards your kayak. After you had thrown your harpoon, you were afraid to follow me any further and so I obtained it without the slightest trouble. I am tired of your story, for every time you tell it, the walrus becomes bigger and bigger until soon you will make me the size of a whale."

For a few moments there was silence, as the tribesmen gazed first at Katerparsuk, then at the skin, and lastly at the harpoon, line and air-bladder. They were astonished, but none so surprised and amazed as the story-teller himself. Then, with one accord, they laughed aloud at the boaster who had told such a wonderful tale of his own bravery, and who was now proved to have been the victim of a clever prank. The baffled and crestfallen hunter hung his head in shame, and slunk away to his own igloo, fearing the further taunts and jeers of his kinsmen.

As for Katerparsuk, he was congratulated on his artful cunning and revenge, and the elders of the tribe admitted him to membership of their council.

(Adapted.)

INTERESTING FACTS
ABOUT
THE ESKIMOS.

1. The Eskimos are the native people of Greenland, and the most northerly parts of Canada and Alaska. We might consider them unattractive in appearance, for they are short, thick-set, with swarthy complexions, flat features, and small narrow eyes. Both men and women allow their hair to grow, as they consider it unlucky to be shorn of their locks.

2. These hardy people are generally coast dwellers, and thus they rely on the sea for their food. They live almost entirely on fish, seal-meat, whale-blubber, and the flesh of sea-birds. Because of their custom of eating their meals uncooked, these northern natives were called **Eskimos,** meaning **Eaters of raw flesh.**

3. Their garments consist of hooded coats, trousers, leggings, and shoes, all made of sealskin, and so thickly are they clad, that they look almost as broad as they are tall. At one time, the Eskimos showed their affection for each other by rubbing noses, but now this practice is seen only when parents caress their children.

4. The Eskimos are clever hunters, and during the summer months, their chief occupation is the slaying of such animals as seals, foxes, caribou and bears. When tracking these creatures, they hide behind white screens, and crawl up close to their quarry. As it is so difficult to spot the much-prized polar bear, a special share is given to the hunter who first sees it. The flesh of these animals is dried, frozen, and stored for use in winter, while the skins which are not needed for domestic purposes, are exchanged for purchases at the trading stations.

5. They are also very skilful fishermen, and venture out on daring expeditions in their frail skin canoes called **kayaks**. The fish are caught by means of lines and hooks, and quite often they manage to kill seals by using spears. When little settlements travel by sea to better hunting grounds they use bigger boats called **umiaks**.

6. In summer the natives live in skin tents called **tupiks**. A thick curtain is hung over the doorway to keep out the cold. In winter they live in **igloos**, which are made of blocks of frozen snow and shaped like bee-hives. Both summer and winter homes are heated and lighted by means of oil-lamps.

7. Even before Columbus discovered America, the fierce Norse Vikings had voyaged to Greenland. For most of the year this huge island of the far North is covered with snow and ice. In the southern part, plants can grow during the very short summer.

8. A most unusual happening takes place each year in this polar region. For a period of about three months in summer, the sun does not set, and for the same length of time in winter, it does not rise.

9. The protective colour of all creatures in the Frozen North is **white**. Amidst snow and ice, a white covering helps the smaller animals to escape the notice of their enemies, while it also enables the larger animals to approach their prey without being detected.

10. From early childhood, the Eskimo children imitate the occupations and pastimes of the grown-ups. A dog-whip is the little boy's first plaything, and training puppy-dogs to draw sledges is a very popular pastime with the young folk. To prevent children from straying too far from home, the parents relate to them many frightful stories of the fierce, vicious polar-bear, and the boys and girls look upon this cruel animal as a kind of " Bogey-man."

QUESTIONS ON THE STORY.

1. Where did this story take place ?
2. Why was Katerparsuk unhappy as a boy ?
3. What was the lad's secret ambition ?
4. How did he learn about hunting wild animals ?
5. What did Katerparsuk decide to make ?
6. What good fortune came his way when he least expected it ?
7. What kind of person was Tutiak ?
8. How did he frighten the orphan boy ?
9. Why did Katerparsuk become a general favourite with the old people of the tribe ?
10. What did he catch on one very dangerous expedition ?
11. How did Katerparsuk make the animal's skin stiff and hard ?
12. Name the chief weapon used in hunting seal and walrus.
13. What was attached to the weapon to make its recovery much easier ?
14. Describe how Katerparsuk tricked his rival.
15. How did the braggart explain the loss of his weapon ?
16. Why did Katerparsuk invite the men of the village to a feast in his igloo ?
17. Why was everyone delighted to accept ?
18. Describe how Katerparsuk had his revenge.
19. What did Tutiak do when he heard how he had been deceived ?
20. How was Katerparsuk rewarded for his artful cunning ?

QUESTIONS ON THE INTERESTING FACTS.

1. Where do the Eskimos live ?
2. What do these hardy people eat ?
3. (a) Describe their general appearance.
   (b) What does the word " Eskimo " mean ?
4. Describe an animal hunt.
5. How do they generally fish ?
6. Describe two types of Eskimo dwellings.
7. Who first discovered Greenland ?

8. What unusual sight may be seen in the Polar Region ?
9. (a) What is the colour of all creatures in the Frozen North ?
   (b) How does this colour protect and help them ?
10. (a) Give any popular pastime of the young folk.
   (b) What creature is looked upon by boys and girls as a kind of " Bogey-man " ?

DEVELOPMENT EXERCISES.

1. Point out on the map the lands inhabited by the Eskimos.
2. Some Eskimos live in Canada. Are they like other Canadians you have seen ? Where do you think the Eskimos came from originally ?
3. Owing to the very cold climate the Eskimos must wear fur clothes. What other people are forced to do the same ?
4. The Eskimos hunt and slay animals in summer and store the meat for use in winter. How is it possible for them to do so ? In what ways do we preserve meat and other foods in this country ?
5. The Eskimos live almost entirely on fish, seal-meat, and whale-blubber. Why do they not have the same kinds of foods as we eat ?
6. Why do the Eskimos build their igloos near the shore ? What double purpose does the oil-lamp serve ? When the inside of a snow-hut is heated, why does it not melt ?
7. The boy in the story built a kayak. How many different kinds of small boats can you name ? Who use them ?
8. The modern Eskimos regularly visit the Canadian trading stations. What goods do you think they request in exchange for their furs ? Give reasons why they ask for these goods.

CROSSING THE LINE

DURING the afternoon, the ship crossed the equator, or "The Line" as the sailors called it. All that morning the older members of the crew had been extremely busy making secret preparations for the reception of Neptune, King of the Five Oceans, Amphitrite, His Queen, and their royal court. A large decorated platform had been erected on deck, and two thrones (tubby chairs covered with red cloth) placed in the centre of the raised stage.

By four o'clock all was ready, and when eight bells had been rung loud shouts of " Ship ahoy ! " startled the ship's company. Suddenly, as if from nowhere, there appeared a gaudily dressed procession consisting of King Neptune, Queen Amphitrite, a physician, a barber and his assistant, and three bears.

The reader will have guessed that all the characters (including the animals) were really sailors in disguise. They walked in slow and solemn state towards the platform, each member of the party with a stern expression on his face, as if the business of the afternoon were a matter of the most serious consequence.

What an imposing figure Neptune made ! His Majesty was dressed in an oilskin jacket and short white trousers, and his bare legs were crossed and recrossed with strips of canvas, which the wearer fondly imagined were quite in the style of the ancient Vikings. He wore a red scarf about his neck and from his shoulders hung a large scarlet quilt. The king had a flowing beard and long hair, and on his head was perched a cardboard crown covered with bright shining tin-foil. The royal Ruler of the Deep bore himself with considerable dignity, as he carried his trident (a gilt wooden fork about six feet long) with one hand, and a large megaphone with the other.

Queen Amphitrite was much more up to date, and did her best to create an impression of beauty and charm. Her hat was a large sombrero, covered with a white scarf and tastefully trimmed with a red silk handkerchief. Her spare figure had become rounded through having her outer garments stuffed with old clothes. She wore a brightly coloured pyjama jacket to represent a blouse, and her skirt consisted of a white bag with the bottom cut out of it. Round her waist was clasped a blue and red elastic belt with a gilt buckle. Her golden hair (manilla rope teased out) hung down her back, and a broad fringe set off her face, which had been thickly powdered with flour. When she walked, the queen's movements could not be termed graceful, as she wore very big boots and took rather large steps. Many of the onlookers concluded that her gait resembled that of the boatswain, who was not to be seen among the spectators.

The physician was a little stout man dressed in a grey suit. He had a bowler hat (several sizes too small) perched jauntily on his head, and carried a black leather bag, which was said to contain cures for all ills.

The barber, who wore a white apron, was heavily laden with the necessary articles of his profession. In one hand, he carried a large bucket, which contained a mixture of grease, pea-soup, oil, and soap. Sticking out of the pail was the handle of the shaving brush which was to apply the lather. (Closer inspection showed it to be a brush generally used for white-washing). In the other hand, he carried a huge wooden razor, which, when fully opened, measured at least five feet.

The barber's assistant also wore a white apron, but although, to judge by his burly figure, he appeared abler than his master to carry loads, it was seen that he was empty-handed.

The three bears wore large rugs which gave them the appearance of cannibals rather than animals.

The procession reached the raised platform, and there the captain received their majesties. Neptune, in a fine baritone voice, sang the usual introduction, beginning :—

> " *I'm Father Neptune, as you see,*
> *And always am in motion,*
> *To intercept the many ships*
> *That sail across my ocean.*"

In three more verses he introduced his queen, the court physician, his barber, and in a fifth and last verse he indicated his royal command that the new sons of Neptune be brought before him.

" *She seems to be a noble ship*
And has some brand new sailors,
So if you'll fetch them all this way
We'll bestow our royal favours."

A whistle was sounded, and at this signal a nearby door opened and twenty members of the crew emerged. They proceeded in Indian file to a place reserved for them in front of the platform and there awaited the royal address. The King, raising his speaking-trumpet to his mouth, read his proclamation :—

" Silence, one and all ! I permit nobody to utter a single word. It is my royal wish and pleasure to hold this court to-day to greet my new subjects. I welcome them to my mighty kingdom, that stretches in all directions to the dim horizon yonder in the distance. I command everyone to be faithful and to respect, honour, and obey all my laws. Let those who hear beware lest they offend or contradict me, for I have the power of life and death over all who dare to disobey or displease me."

As Father Neptune finished this speech he removed his crown and wig, and wiped his glossy, bald head. The spectators roared with laughter and applauded with great gusto. The King acknowledged their cheers, and then called on the first applicant to step forward. He was a young stoker, and this was his first voyage. Many questions were fired at him, but he managed to answer them to Neptune's satisfaction. The Sea Monarch declared that, as the lad's father was one of his most respected subjects, he would be treated with the greatest courtesy. This, however, did not prevent him from being duly lathered and shaved, after a pill, made of soap and of dripping rolled in flour, had been administered by the doctor.

" I've finished with this applicant, Your Majesty," the barber announced as he wiped his razor on his white apron.

" Neptune," said Queen Amphitrite, " I think this young stranger has had enough."

" As you wish, my dear," replied her husband. He waved his hand majestically, and at this pre-arranged signal the barber's assistant sprang forward and pushed the surprised victim into a tarpaulin full of sea-water. The bears, growling fiercely, ducked him three times, and then allowed him to scramble out. The lad immediately dashed off to his quarters, and changing into dry clothes, soon returned to enjoy the antics of the other applicants.

One by one, each member of the crew was pitched into the bath and well soused. Each candidate emerged from the bath a true son of Neptune—a genuine deep-water sailors. Sometimes, if an applicant resisted the attentions of the barber or doctor, five duckings were ordered instead of three. It was harmless fun and excellent fooling, and was thoroughly enjoyed by all.

The ceremony over, King Neptune gave a short farewell address, in which he complimented the captain on his crew and his ship. His Majesty then called on his retainers to return with him to the deep—but the spectators noted that they proceeded in the direction of the galley.

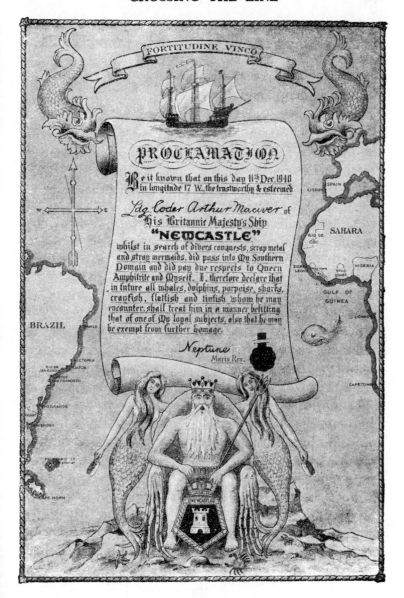

At supper, that same evening, the captain (by order of Neptune) presented certificates to those who had passed the test and become subjects of his kingdom. The recipients were called upon to perform an item of entertainment, and their efforts were greeted with much applause.

Here is an extract from the official bulletin regarding the visit of King George VI and Queen Elizabeth (then Duke and Duchess of York) to Australia in 1927.

" Dosed with a pill of dough and dripping, lathered with soap of sinister origin, shaved with a large wooden razor, and subjected to a three times ducking by Neptune's bears—His Royal Highness was initiated into the " Order of the Old Sea Dog " as the ship crossed the Line. Her Royal Highness, in different and gentler ceremony, was invested with the insignia of the " Order of the Golden Mermaid."

It is interesting to discover that two new orders for those who brave the trials of the Far North have been instituted. In the first, the King of the Seas has apparently extended the rule of his trident by granting " The Order of the Bluenose " to the gallant sailors who cross the Arctic Circle. This certificate is signed, not only by Neptunus Rex, but also by " Aurora Borealis, Queen of His Majesty's Northern Provinces." The second order, which is the American equivalent of the first, proclaims that the recipient has crossed the Arctic Circle and entered the " Domain of the Polar Bear." For obvious reasons, there are no ceremonies such as that of " Crossing the Line" attached to these two orders.

INTERESTING FACTS
ABOUT
SHIPS AND CUSTOMS AT SEA.

1. The body or hull of a ship is built in a **shipyard**. At the launching ceremony it is the custom for a lady to name the vessel and break a bottle of wine against its side. The ship is then engined and furnished at a **fitting-out basin**. The first journey is called the " **maiden** " voyage. When in need of cleaning and repairs a ship proceeds to a **dry-dock**.

2. (*a*) The **bow** is the front part of the ship and the **stern** is the rear or back part. On the vessel's bow is its name in large letters, while on the stern the name and port of registry are shown.

(*b*) **Port** is the left side of the ship (looking forward), and shows a red light at night. **Starboard** is

the right side of the ship (looking forward), and shows a green light at night.

3. (*a*) Ships have **Roman numbers** painted on their bows. These figures are a foot apart and start from the bottom, so that one can tell at a glance how much of the ship is under water.

(*b*) On a ship's side is painted a small circle with a horizontal line through it, and no ship is allowed to load so that this line is below water. This mark is called the **Plimsoll Line,** and is named after Samuel Plimsoll, who caused an Act of Parliament to be passed against the overloading of ships.

4. The captain or master is often referred to as the " skipper " or " **old man** " ; the wireless operator as " **sparks** " ; the carpenter as " **chips** " ; the cook as " **doctor** " ; the sailor who works the loading engines as the " **donkey-man** " ; and an old sailor who has had experience of sailing ships as a " **shellback**." Certain nicknames for men with particular surnames are quite common, *e.g.* Clark—" **Nobby**," Miller—

" Dusty," Wilson—" Tug," Murray—" Tiddler," Mac-
Donald (or any Scottish surname) —" Jock," Jones
(or any Welsh surname)—" Taffy," O'Connor (or
any Irish surname)—" Pat."

5. We would expect a ship to be referred to as
" it," but instead we always say " she," The high
platform for the captain is called the **bridge**;
the look-out post on the fore-mast—the " **crow's
nest** "; the cook-house—the **galley**; a floor—a
deck; a passage—an **alley-way**; a stair—a **companion-
way**; a small room—a **cabin**; a bed—a **bunk**; a
small rope—a **painter**; and the movable bridge to
allow passengers to get aboard or go ashore—the
gangway.

6. Every ship has a diary which is known as the
log. In this book are recorded the ship's progress
and all matters of interest. The ship's day of 24 hours
is divided into spells of duty called **watches**. These
watches are all of 4 hours each, except the " **dog
watches**," which are from 4 to 6 p.m. and 6 to 8,
p.m. A bell is rung for each half-hour of the watch
thus giving a final eight bells to an ordinary watch
and a final four bells to a dog-watch. To welcome
the New Year, the youngest member of the crew is
given the privilege of striking sixteen bells at midnight
on 31st December.

7. Ships very seldom commence a voyage on a
Friday, and particularly on Friday the thirteenth of a
month, as it is considered unlucky by sailors. While
at sea, it is thought to be an ill-omen to harm or kill
sea-birds; to use the word " rabbit "; to hear the

clinking of glasses; or to whistle a tune. On the other hand it is said to be lucky if a black cat strays aboard and makes its home on a ship, or if a school of porpoises follows a vessel.

8. A cargo or passenger ship always lowers or "dips" her flag in salute to a warship. All steam-ships must give the right-of-way to sailing ships. A vessel's flag is flown at half-mast as a sign of mourning. The international wireless signal of a ship in distress is "S O S." Ships and cargoes are generally insured against damage or loss by rough weather, fire, fog, hidden reefs, and icebergs. The greatest ship-insurance company in the world is **Lloyd's** in London. When special announcements are made, the famous Lutine Bell (taken from a ship-wreck and now hanging in Lloyd's Exchange) is rung. The expression "**A 1 at Lloyd's**" is used to indicate a ship in first class condition.

9. The **three white lines** on a navyman's light blue collar are often said to refer to Nelson's three great victories — Copenhagen, Nile, and Trafalgar — but actually these collar stripes are merely ornamental. When introduced in 1857 there were only two stripes, but later a third was added. The **black silk scarf**, which every sailor wears, is thought by some people to be a token of mourning for Nelson, but the neckerchief, often spotted or coloured, was worn before the days of Britain's greatest admiral. In the early days it was usually worn around the head to prevent sweat from running into the eyes.

10. The common phrase "**The Seven Seas**" refers to the five oceans, the Atlantic, Pacific, Indian, Arctic,

and Antarctic, with the Atlantic divided into North Atlantic and South Atlantic, and the Pacific divided into North Pacific and South Pacific. " The High Seas " refers to all parts of the sea not under the control of neighbouring countries. To sail " **before the mast** " means to work aboard a ship as an ordinary member of the crew. The reason for this expression was that the forecastle or " fo'c'sle," which was the crew's quarters, was situated at the bow and therefore in front of the mast.

QUESTIONS ON THE STORY.

1. Where and when did the ceremony of " Crossing the Line " take place ?
2. How many were in Neptune's party ?
3. Name the various members of the party.
4. What kingdom did Neptune rule ?
5. At what time did the ceremony begin ?
6. Describe King Neptune.
7. How was Queen Amphitrite dressed ?
8. What did the doctor carry ?
9. Describe the barber's instruments.
10. What did the three " bears " look like ?
11. Who received the party on board ship ?
12. Who was the first applicant to step forward ?
13. How did the doctor treat him ?
14. What did the barber do ?
15. Who pushed the applicant into the tarpaulin full of sea-water ?
16. How many times was the lad ducked ?

17. What did those who had passed the test receive at supper that same evening ?

18. What were the recipients called upon to do ?

19. Name two other " Sea Orders."

20. To whom are they granted ?

QUESTIONS ON THE INTERESTING FACTS.

1. (a) Where is a ship (1) built, (2) engined and furnished, (3) cleaned and repaired ?

   (b) What is a ship's first journey called ?

2. (a) What is the meaning of (1) bow, (2) stern, (3) amidships ?

   (b) Which side of a ship is (1) port, (2) starboard, and what colour of light is shown on each side at night ?

3. (a) Why do ships have Roman numerals painted on their bows ?

   (b) Where would you look for a ship's name ?

4. What is the Plimsoll Line and why is it so called ?

5. What terms do sailors use for (a) a wireless operator, (b) a carpenter, (c) a man whose surname is Clark, (d) a Welshman, (e) a cook-house, (f) a stair, (g) a bed, (h) a rope ?

6. (a) What name is given to a ship's diary ?

   (b) What are spells of duty called ?

   (c) When are the " dog " watches ?

7. Sailors are said to be very superstitious. Give two supposed indications of (a) ill-omen, (b) future good fortune.

8. (a) What is the sign of mourning on board ship ?

   (b) What is the international wireless signal of a ship in distress ?

   (c) How are ships usually lost or damaged ?

9. Give the reason for (a) the three white stripes on a navyman's blue collar, (b) the black silk kerchief.

10. What is meant by (a) The Seven Seas, (b) The High Seas ?

DEVELOPMENT EXERCISES.

1. Point out on the map (*a*) the Equator or " Line," (*b*) the Arctic Circle, (*c*) the Seven Seas.

2. Make a fairly large drawing of a liner with two funnels. Below it name as many parts as you can—*e.g.* bow, deck, bridge, etc.

3. How many different kinds of ships can you name and for what purpose is each kind generally used ? Example:— yacht . . . pleasure sailing.

4. A rider or driver guides his horse by means of the reins. How does (*a*) a driver guide his motor-car, (*b*) a pilot guide his aeroplane, (*c*) a captain guide his ship ?

5. The captain is in command of a ship. What particular name is given to the person in charge of (*a*) a school, (*b*) an orchestra, (*c*) a workshop, (*d*) a newspaper, (*e*) an army, (*f*) a republic ?

6. A ship's flag is flown at half-mast as a sign of mourning. Give various signs by which you know people who are in mourning.

7. A ship sends out the message " S O S " when in distress. What would you do (*a*) if you lost your way, (*b*) if you sprained your ankle, (*c*) if your sister's. dress caught fire, (*d*) if you noticed an escape of gas in the house ?

8. Neptune and Amphitrite, the Roman god and goddess of the sea, are characters in the story. Can you name any other gods and goddesses of whom you have heard or read ?

THE SHIPS

FOR many a year I've watched the
    ships a-sailing to and fro,
The mighty ships, the little ships, the
    speedy and the slow ;
And many a time I've told myself that
    some day I would go
Around the world that is so full of wonders.

The swift and stately liners, how they run
    without a rest :
The great three-masters, they have touched
    the East and told the West :
The monster burden-bearers—oh, they all
    have plunged and pressed
Around the world that is so full of wonders.

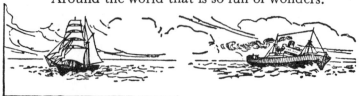

The shabby tramp that like a wedge is
 hammered through the seas,
The little brown-sailed brigantine that traps
 the lightest breeze—
Oh, I'd be well content to fare aboard the
 least of these
Around the world that is so full of wonders.

❧

The things I've heard, the things I've read,
 the things I've dreamed might be,
The boyish tales, the old men's yarns—
 they will not pass from me :
I've heard, I've read, I've dreamed—but
 all the time I've longed to see—
Around the world that is so full of wonders.

❧

So year by year I watch the ships a-sailing
 to and fro,
The ships that come as strangers and the
 ships I've learned to know—
Folks smile to hear me say that some
 day I will go
Around the world that is so full of wonders.

J. J. BELL.

THE ORIGIN OF OUR NUMBERS

IN very early times people used sticks to represent numbers, *e.g.*

These numerals, which we inherited from the Arabs, have been called the Arabic system, although the figures were invented not in Arabia, but in India. They were not of much use until the Arabs introduced the zero (O), and made possible a place value in figures.

As the first system to use numbers, exactly as we use them nowadays, consisted of numbers **drawn** on boards covered with sand—it was called the Gobar or Dust system.

1234567890

The Romans used letters of the alphabet for numbers, and their system was probably based on the numbers of human fingers.

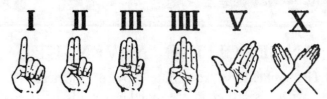

C, representing a hundred, is the initial letter of Centum. The sign was originally ▢ and half of ▢ became ∟, which is used to represent fifty. D, used for five hundred, is half of Φ (M)—the initial letter of Mille—a thousand.

I = 1, II = 2, III = 3, IIII = 4, V = 5, X = 10, L = 50, C = 100, D = 500, M = 1000.

AN EXCITING ADVENTURE

RIP, a healthy, strapping boy of fourteen, lived with his father in the northern wilds of Canada, not far from the shores of Hudson Bay. Their home, a low-built log-cabin, lay in a forest clearing and the surrounding trees afforded protection from the snow-storms and the icy blasts of the wind. Rip's father had come to this cold, lonely part of the country to earn his livelihood by hunting and trapping wild animals for their furs.

It was certainly a fine, free, open-air life, and Rip thoroughly enjoyed exploring the ravines, streams, and immense forests of red pine, ash, poplar, spruce, oak, and birch trees. He and his father were usually too busy and too interested in their work to feel lonely in this out-of-the-way place. Rip was familiar with the habits of all the wild creatures, and his father often complimented him on setting the traps so cunningly that the victims did not notice them until too late. In the neighbouring forests lived such wild animals as the bear, beaver, stoat, fox, marten, otter, and, last but not least, the wolf.

Winter had set in, and this was their busiest season, as the coats of the animals became specially thick to withstand the extreme cold. The fur trapper and his son had already caught and carefully skinned several stoats and foxes, and their valuable pelts were stored in the cabin until they collected sufficient furs to take to the nearest trading station some fifteen miles away.

One day Rip and his father went out on their usual morning round of the traps. To save time, they separated and each trudged through the snow noting carefully any fresh footprints. Suddenly Rip heard a shout and he quickly retraced his steps to the spot where he had left his father. Imagine his horror when he found him lying groaning on the ground, having been badly mauled by a bear.

The boy, with great difficulty, carried his father back to the cabin and did what he could to relieve the pain of his wounds. He was quick to realise that he must obtain help as soon as he possibly could. The short cut to the trading post lay by way of the Great Fish River, which, fortunately, was frozen over. Seizing his skates, he made his way to the river bank and was soon gliding swiftly over the ice in the direction of the station.

From the forest that lined the shores of the river a long, eerie howl rang out on the frosty air. It was a sound that made Rip's heart quail within him, for it was the dreaded cry of the most cruel and cunning creature in the North—the wolf. Rip knew too, that like all the other creatures of the wild, the wolves were experiencing the famine of winter and were becoming bold with hunger. They formed into packs and roamed the country, heedless of danger in their desperation to obtain food.

With beating heart Rip glanced from side to side as he skated down the river. He saw the grey, gaunt shapes of several wolves slinking among the trees. Out of the woods they came and on to the ice. One, bolder than the others, suddenly leaped from among the rest and shot across in front of him, its jaws snapping wickedly as it narrowly missed him. This incident seemed to

give him added strength, and he flung every ounce of energy into his effort to escape. From either side the wolves closed in behind him, howling and yelping with excitement as they raced after their quarry. With gasping breath and pounding heart the boy skated as he had never skated before. There was no escape for him if he tried to gain either bank, and, having no weapon of any kind, he could use nothing but his skill as a skater against the attack of the merciless pack.

After some considerable distance, with the wolves still in close pursuit, the boy felt that he was beginning to tire. It was the first time that year that he had used skates, and his muscles were aching with the unaccustomed exercise. His pace became a trifle slower, but still he managed to keep slightly ahead of the snarling wolves. As the boy raced over the ice he thought to himself that it was just a matter of time until the pursuing pack overtook him.

All at once he heard a sound which caused him to gasp—the thunder of falling water. Rip then realised that he was nearing the high river falls. Over a sheer cliff of nearly a hundred feet they fell, and apparently the frost had not been severe enough to freeze them. Suddenly an idea struck him and he purposely slackened speed until the howling brutes were only a yard or two away. Straight for the falls he headed, with the wind singing in his ears and the cold spray dashing into his face. The animals followed, intent on their prey and quite oblivious of approaching danger.

The boy could discern the edge of the falls through the mist of water-vapour ahead and he allowed the

pack to come closer until they were practically at his heels. Onwards he sped and when only a few feet from the brink, he wheeled sharply to the left and dashed towards the bank. The wolves, just behind him and confident of overtaking their quarry, tried to pull up but in vain. They clawed frantically at the ice, but, owing to their speed and the slippery foothold, they were unable to stop and shot over the precipice.

Scarcely believing that he had escaped, the boy staggered to the bank and sat down, trembling in every limb. When he had recovered a little, Rip resumed his journey across rough country and was almost exhausted by the time he reached his destination. On arrival at the trading post, he told of his father's plight and an urgent message for medical aid was sent by wireless to the nearest town, some two hundred miles away.

After a well-earned rest Rip, accompanied by two trapper friends of his father, set out on the homeward journey. They travelled by sleigh, drawn by hardy Alsatian huskies, and a few hours later they arrived at the little, lonely cabin in the clearing. Immediately, the men, in their rough and ready fashion, did what they could to relieve the suffering of the injured man.

Before long they heard the drone of the aeroplane, which was bringing a doctor in answer to their summons. A signal fire was lit and the smoke guided the pilot to a safe landing. The doctor alighted from the 'plane and at once gave Rip's father skilled medical treatment. After an operation, which proved very successful, he stated that there was no doubt that the boy, by his gallant action, had saved his father's life. The story of Rip's heroism quickly spread throughout the trading posts and his exciting adventure was often recounted.

Adapted from " Let Her Rip," by Arthur Minter.

INTERESTING FACTS ABOUT CANADA.

1. Leaving out of account that in early times the Vikings crossed the Atlantic Ocean and visited many parts of North America, it may be said that **John** and **Sebastian Cabot** discovered Canada in 1497 A.D. The French were the first settlers in this great country, and the word **Canada** comes from the Red Indian language ; "**Kannata**," meaning "a number of huts."

2. Canada, known as the "**Land of the Maple Leaf**" or the "**Land of Promise**," is a member of the British Commonwealth of Nations. It was added to the British Empire as a result of General Wolfe's victory over the French forces at **Quebec** in 1759 A.D. The country is divided into provinces, each having its own capital and laws. These provinces send a number of members to the Dominion Parliament in **Ottawa**, the capital of Canada. There are many fine cities such as Toronto, Winnipeg, Montreal, Quebec, Halifax and Vancouver.

3. As the country extends for thousands of miles from the Arctic Ocean to the United States and from the Atlantic Ocean to the Pacific Ocean, all kinds of weather conditions are to be found there. One part of the border with the United States is along a line of latitude known as the "**49th Parallel**," and most of the other part is

formed by Lakes Superior, Huron, Erie, Michigan and Ontario which are popularly known as " The Lakes." Time, according to the sun, changes by one hour every fifteen degrees of longitude so that it is necessary in Canada to have four standard times—**Eastern** time, **Prairie** time, **Mountain** time, and **Pacific** time.

4. Various methods of transport, from the sledge drawn by huskies to the modern air-liner, are to be seen in this huge country. The most important link across Canada is the famous Canadian Pacific Railway, better known by its initials **C.P.R.** A journey across Canada takes several days. The trains have day cars, observation cars, dining cars and sleeping cars, and there are many attendants to look after the comfort of the passengers.

5. **Lumbering** is the name given to the work of cutting down trees and sawmilling them into logs. In winter, the **lumberjacks** fell the trees, lop off the branches, and place the trunks on sledges to be dragged to the

nearest suitable river. When spring comes, the tree-trunks are formed into huge rafts and floated down the river to the saw-mills. Not only planks and boards are made from the timber, much of it is used in producing wood-pulp for paper-making.

6. **Fishing** is a very important industry. In the western rivers of Canada, immense quantities of salmon are caught and sent, in tins, to all parts of the world. It is said, " They eat all they can, and they can all they can't." On the Atlantic seaboard, the island of **Newfoundland** (adjacent to and now a part of Canada) was our first colony, and is famous for its cod and herring fishing. This great fishing ground is often covered with heavy fog, due to the meeting of the cold currents from Greenland with the warm currents from the south.

7. In central Canada, there is a vast plain known as the **Prairie,** and this region produces more wheat and corn than any other part of the world. The farms are so big that the houses are miles apart and nobody goes to the expense of fencing. The farm-houses are heated by basement furnaces with pipes to carry the heat to every room. Owing to the long distances between neighbours and friends, each family usually has a telephone and motor car.

8. The many forests of northern Canada are the homes of numerous wild animals, such as the bear, stoat (ermine), muskrat (musquash), marten (sable), mink, beaver, and fox. As these creatures have valuable furs, trapping is an important occupation. The **Hudson Bay Company** was started as long ago as 1670, and this famous firm has trading stations in many parts of the

country. At these lonely outposts, the trappers sell their furs or exchange them for goods.

9. Law and order is maintained in the prairies and barren lands by a fine body of men in scarlet and blue uniforms, who are known to everyone as the **Royal Canadian Mounted Police (R.C.M.P.)** or "Mounties." These " Watchdogs of the Prairies," as they are sometimes called, have earned a splendid reputation for bravery and devotion to duty, and criminals seldom escape them.

10. The grandeur of Canada's scenery is well-known, especially of such places as the **Niagara Falls**, the **Rocky Mountains** and the **Canadian National Parks.** The people take full advantage of their surroundings to enjoy sport and recreation—camping and canoeing in the summer, and sledging, skiing, and skating in the winter. **Ice-hockey** may be said to be the national sport.

QUESTIONS ON THE STORY.

1. Where is the scene of the story ?
2. What age was Rip ?
3. How did his father earn his living ?

4. Name some of the trees which grew in the forests.
5. Name some of the animals which lived in the neighbourhood.
6. Why was winter the busiest season?
7. How far away was the trading station?
8. How did Rip's father receive his serious injuries?
9. After taking his father home, what did the boy decide to do?
10. As it was winter, what was the short cut to the trading station?
11. How did Rip hope to get there quickly?
12. While the boy was on his way for help, what did he hear?
13. What did these cruel, hungry animals do?
14. Describe how Rip outwitted the pack of wolves.
15. What did they do at the station when he arrived?
16. By what means did he travel back to the cabin?
17. Who accompanied him?
18. How did help arrive?
19. How was the pilot guided to a safe landing?
20. What did the doctor say?

QUESTIONS ON THE INTERESTING FACTS.

1. (a) Who are credited with the discovery of Canada?
   (b) What is said to be the origin of the word "Canada"?
2. (a) Give a popular name for Canada.
   (b) Where was the final battle between the British and French fought?
   (c) Name the leader of the British forces.
3. How is the country divided and governed?
4. (a) What is the name given to the land border-line between Canada and the United States?
   (b) Name various methods of transport to be seen in this huge country.
   (c) What is the most important link across Canada?
5. Describe the lumber industry.
6. Name the most important fisheries.
7. What is the Prairie?
8. (a) Name five wild animals hunted for their valuable pelts.

(*b*) What famous firm has trading stations in all parts of the country?

9. Who maintain law and order in the lonely regions?

10. (*a*) Name two places of outstanding natural beauty.

(*b*) How do the people enjoy themselves (1) in summer, (2) in winter?

(*c*) What is the national sport?

DEVELOPMENT EXERCISES.

1. Point out on the map (*a*) the northern wilds of Canada, (*b*) the prairie land of Canada, (*c*) Hudson Bay.

2. In the extreme north west there is a state which does not belong to Canada. What is its name? To whom does it belong?

3. The trappers sell their furs at the trading stations, and from there, the pelts are sent to be sold in the markets of the big cities. To what uses are furs put?

4. The poet, Rudyard Kipling, referred to Canada as " Our Lady of the Snows." Do you think this is a good title? State why.

5. What qualities of character and physique do you think are needed to become a " Mountie? "

6. All of us eat some food which comes from Canada. Name (*a*) a fruit, (*b*) fish, and (*c*) cereal which Canada sends us.

7. What season in Canada is known as " the fall? " Can you tell why it is given that name?

8. If you study a map of Canada, you will find a great number of names of British people and places. How do you explain this?

MORGAN THE BUCCANEER

HENRY MORGAN was born in Wales in 1635. As a youth he spent much of his time at the port of Bristol, gambling, brawling and getting into trouble. Later, he spent seven years in Barbados, and in 1660 came to Jamaica and joined the buccaneers in Port Royal. In five years he rose to become their leader.

The buccaneers were men from every nation, but mainly French, English and Dutch. They lived peace· fully in Hispaniola where they hunted wild cattle and pigs, and supplied meat, hides and tallow to passing ships in exchange for ammunition. Their dress was a coarse shirt, short trousers, raw-hide shoes and a hat with short brim except where it shaded the eyes. Their clothing was so blood-stained that it seemed blackened as with tar. They carried knives and a powder horn in their belts and bullets in their pockets. They usually worked in pairs, each man having a partner with whom everything was shared. Although these hunters harmed no one, the Spaniards tried to drive them out of Hispaniola by killing off the animals they hunted. The buccaneers then moved to the island of Tortuga and

from there they carried out their revenge against the
Spaniards. In their low, fast vessels they attacked
Spanish ships in the Caribbean, killing sailors and looting
the treasures. In Port Royal they found a ready market
for their loot, a safe place to repair ships and oppor-
tunities for amusing themselves, and so they flocked
to the port in large numbers.

One day in January, 1688, Henry Morgan, the
buccaneer leader, went to see the Governor, Sir Thomas
Modyford. He asked to speak to the Governor alone.

"I have brought you very alarming news, Your
Excellency," said Morgan.

Governor Modyford knew Morgan well. He knew
Morgan was a buccaneer. He knew of the life of violence
he lived in Port Royal whenever he returned from
attacking the Spanish ships.

"I have heard," said Morgan, "that the Spaniards
are gathering a powerful fleet off the coast of Cuba. I
am sure you can think of the reason for that."

The Governor turned pale as Morgan spoke. England and Spain were at war, and news of a Spanish fleet in the Caribbean could only mean that plans were being made to attack Jamaica.

" It is plain that the Spaniards intend to attack Port Royal," Morgan continued. " Our only hope is to prevent their doing so."

" How can that be done? " Modyford asked. " I have no fleet to match theirs nor are my soldiers able to meet them in battle."

" You must depend on the buccaneers," replied Morgan. " We are the only ones who can help you at this time. My men are experienced in battling with the Spanish sailors. We will destroy the Spanish fleet and save Port Royal. To do this you must grant me a commission."

At this the Governor could not hide his fears. He hesitated in granting a commission to the riotous buccaneer, but there was nothing else to do. He therefore decided to grant the commission and signed the document.

Two days later the ships of the buccaneers, with Morgan in command, sailed to attack the Spaniards at Puerto Principe in Cuba. They were joined by some English and French ships. In four hours the Spaniards were totally defeated and many of them killed. Morgan ordered that those who were still alive should be assembled and compelled to tell where they had hidden their money. Those who refused to tell were tortured. Morgan and his men collected a great quantity of loot. On his return to Port Royal with the booty, Morgan was given a hero's welcome.

He next planned to conquer Porto Bello on the isthmus

of Panama. This was one of the strongest Spanish defences in the Caribbean. Morgan knew this would be a stiff battle so he did not tell his men until the last moment where the attack would be. The buccaneers took strong objection to this.

" We shall all be killed," they said. " Our numbers are too few to fight against the large Spanish army stationed at Porto Bello." Morgan encouraged them and told them of the great wealth to be found in Porto Bello. " If our number is small our hearts are great, and the fewer we are the more we can work together, and each person will have a bigger share in the loot," he said.

The buccaneers decided to follow their leader and launch the attack. At dusk that evening their ships drew near to Porto Bello. Their army of about four hundred and eighty men landed and moved quietly into the forest behind the city for an overland march. The people of Porto Bello had heard that the buccaneers were coming against them and many took refuge in

La Gloria Castle carrying their treasures with them. From the castle they opened fire on the buccaneers and the battle began. Morgan succeeded in defeating the Spaniards and capturing the castle.

The buccaneers could not restrain their greed when they saw the great wealth the Spaniards had. They tore ear-rings from the ears of women and hacked off the fingers of others to get the valuable rings they wore. They took 250,000 pieces of eight, besides gems, costly silks, linen and other merchandise.

Encouraged by this successful attack, Morgan prepared for his next venture without delay. This was to attack Maracaibo, an important seaport in Venezuela. He overcame the large Spanish fleet by sending fire ships among them. He and his men then marched into the city and demanded a large sum of money. The Spaniards paid to save their city from destruction.

Morgan next planned to attack Panama by way of the Chagres river. The river was shallow in parts, and the ships could not sail up to the city. The buccaneer army was therefore compelled to complete the journey by land. They marched through marshes and forests. Many of the men died on the march. Some were attacked by alligators; some were bitten by poisonous snakes and some contracted malaria. With the remnant of his army, however, Morgan sacked Panama.

The Spanish ambassador in London sought to punish Morgan for the attack on Panama. He wanted Morgan to be executed, but King Charles of England blamed Governor Modyford, who had commissioned him. King Charles ordered that Governor Modyford should be arrested, and appointed Sir Thomas Lynch Lieutenant-Governor of Jamaica. Lynch was determined to put an end to the activities of the buccaneers. He arrested Morgan and sent him as a prisoner to England to be tried there. He was freed after his trial. It was shown that Morgan's activity as a buccaneer was intended to save the British colony of Jamaica from the Spaniards, and that he acted lawfully because he was commissioned by Governor Modyford.

Later Morgan was knighted and in 1674 the King appointed him Lieutenant-Governor of Jamaica. As Governor he turned against his former companions and drove the buccaneers from Port Royal.

INTERESTING FACTS
ABOUT
LIGHTHOUSES.

1. Lighthouses are special buildings erected around the coast to serve as beacons by night and as landmarks by day. Though they differ in size and appearance, most of them are built in the form of a **high tower** resembling the trunk of a large tree.

2. These friends of the mariners are situated on headlands, high cliffs, islands, and lonely reefs ; in fact, on any place where they can best serve the purpose of warning and guiding ships. Even on sandbanks, where a lighthouse cannot be built, notice of danger is given by a **lightship** at anchor.

3. The following is the lighthouse keeper's first duty : —" You are to light the lamps every evening at sunsetting, and keep them constantly burning, bright and clear, till sunrising."

4. Originally, bonfires and large iron baskets with lit fuel were placed on dangerous rocks to warn ships. In these earlier days some shipwrecks were caused by wicked people shifting or extinguishing the beacons so that they could plunder the cargoes of the unfortunate vessels.

5. As many of the lighthouses are on lonely islands and perilous rocks, the task of supplying food regularly

SECTION OF LIGHTHOUSE

EXPLOSIVE FOG SIGNAL
LAMP ROOM
SERVICE ROOM
STORES
BEDROOM
LIVING ROOM
OIL ROOM
STORES
WATER TANKS

BUOY LIGHT

LIGHT SHIP

NORE

FOG SIRENS

LIGHT STAKE

to these outposts is a hazardous adventure, especially
in stormy weather. Generally, provisions and the men
to relieve those on duty are taken to the " Sentinels of
the Deep " every fortnight by a lighthouse service ship.

6. Lighthouses which show a steady constant light
without change are called " Fixed Lights." Most lighthouses, however, flash at certain intervals and each
has its own distinctive signal.

7. The flashing light does not mean that the light
goes out and in. The lantern revolves round the lamp
and certain parts of the lantern have special glass
which acts like a mirror and reflects the light back to
a " bull's eye." When these lantern reflectors face in
your direction the light appears to be out, and when
the " bull's eye " shines towards you, the light appears
at its brightest.

8. The thick powerful lenses of the lantern cause
the light to shine a great distance over the sea, and the
signal or beam may be seen as far as twenty miles
away. During the day, the blinds inside the lantern
are drawn, because the sun's rays penetrating the lenses
would heat and melt parts of the lamp.

9. When visibility is poor owing to fog or mist,
other methods of warning ships are necessary. At
some lighthouses guns are fired, at others bells are
rung, but at most, fog-horns are sounded.

10. The Pharos Lighthouse, built in 330 B.C. at
Alexandria in Egypt, was the first lighthouse, and was
considered one of the Seven Wonders of the Ancient
World. Stromboli, a volcano in the Lipari Islands
(Italy), is often referred to as " The Lighthouse of the
Mediterranean "

QUESTIONS ON THE STORY

1. Where was Henry Morgan born? When did he arrive in Jamaica?
2. Where did the buccaneers first settle? How did they live?
3. Who drove the buccaneers from their first settlement? How did the buccaneers take their revenge?
4. What news did Morgan bring to the Governor of Jamaica one day in 1688?
5. Where did Morgan first gain a victory over his enemies?
6. Where was the next attack made? Why did Morgan's men object at first? How did Morgan encourage them?
7. What means did Morgan use to destroy the enemy fleet off Maracaibo? The city paid him a large sum to avoid plunder and destruction. What is such a sum called?
8. What dangers and difficulties did Morgan and his men encounter during the march on Panama?
9. Tell what happened to Morgan on his return from Panama.
10. What honours were later bestowed on Morgan? Can you think of some reasons why Morgan then drove the buccaneers out of Port Royal?

QUESTIONS ON THE INTERESTING FACTS

1. What is the purpose of a lighthouse ?
2. Where are lighthouses to be found ?
3. What is a lighthouse keeper's first duty ?
4. How were ships warned of danger in olden time ?
5. How are the " Lonely Sentinels of the Deep " relieved and provisioned ?
6. What is meant by a " Fixed Light " ?
7. Explain how a flashing light operates.
8. What causes the light to shine a great distance ?
9. How are ship's warned when visibility is poor ?
10. (a) Which was the first known lighthouse ?
    (b) What is known as "The Lighthouse of the Mediterranean" ?

DEVELOPMENT EXERCISES.

1. The lights from lighthouses warn ships of danger and keep them safely away from the rocks. At busy street crossings there are lights to warn people of traffic danger. What do the colours red, amber, and green mean?

2. At important lighthouses, three or four men take turns of duty on the light. What might happen if a lighthouse keeper neglected his duty?

3. Lighthouses plan an important part in safeguarding the lives of all seamen. In what circumstances would the following be used:—life-jacket, life-buoy, ship's life-boat, breeches buoy, shore stationed life-boat?

4. Railways also have a system of light signals to protect passengers and trains. How does an engine-driver know (a) that there is danger ahead, (b) that it is safe to proceed? What signals are used in fog?

5. Apart from lights, there are many road-signs to warn motorists of approaching danger. Can you describe any such signs?

6. Morgan sent fire ships among the Spanish fleet. Why would the Spanish ships burn easily? What are ships made of nowadays?

7. The Spanish ships were large, three-decked sailing vessels. What were such ships called? Can you name any other ships of olden days?

8. Sailing ships were often blown off course by unfavourable winds. Here are some names of the wind. Place them in order from the lightest to the strongest: hurricane, moderate wind, gale, light breeze, storm, strong wind.

THE SECRET TREASURE

MANY years ago, in the country of Holland, there lived a hard-working peasant named Hans Bloom and his very talkative wife Nanette. They stayed in a small but comfortable little cottage on the outskirts of a village, and Hans, who was what we would now call a crofter or smallholder, earned his living by cultivating a few fields, snaring game in the neighbouring woods, and fishing in the nearby river.

One lovely spring morning, as Hans was ploughing in a corner of his largest field, the plough-share struck something hard, which brought him to a sudden halt. On looking at the cause of the stoppage, he uttered a cry of amazement, for the obstacle was not a boulder as he expected, but a large metal box, half-hidden in the earth. After looking round to see that no one was watching him, Hans dug round the box until he had completely unearthed it. He then placed it on the ground and tried to force the lid with his knife, but without success. However, by smashing the lock with a stone, he managed to open it and see the contents.

Imagine his surprise and joy, on discovering that the box was almost full of gold and silver coins. He kept staring and staring at the treasure, as if he could scarcely believe his eyes. But, after the first moments of delight had passed, he frowned as he began to wonder what he should do in order to retain his newly-found wealth. The chief difficulty was that he must tell his wife Nanette, and she, being one of the village gossips, could not possibly keep a secret for long. The news would soon reach the ears of the Count, who was the overlord of the district, and he, no doubt, would immediately confiscate the treasure and punish him into the bargain, for not informing him in the first place. Hans closed and replaced the box in the hole, taking good care to cover it well, lest it might be seen by anyone who chanced to come that way. He then sat for a long time, with his head cupped in his hands, trying to think of a plan by which he could keep the treasure. Suddenly he sprang to his feet exclaiming, " Of course! The very thing ! " Going over to the plough, he quickly unyoked the ass, and led the creature to its small stable at the back of the house.

Nanette was surprised to see her husband return from work so early in the day, and, when he told her of his wonderful luck, she was overjoyed, and at once began to talk of the many things they would buy with the money. Hans made her promise not to reveal his discovery to anyone, not even to their dearest friends, and this vow she readily made at least half-a-dozen times in her excitement. Despite her repeated promises, however, Hans knew that the story of his good fortune would soon be the talk of the whole neighbourhood.

An hour or so later, Hans decided to put his plan into operation, and went to the wood where he had set his snares. To his great satisfaction, he found that a fine hare had been caught in one of his traps. Removing the dead animal from the snare, he placed it in his bag, and proceeded to the river, where he drew in his fishing lines. Certainly luck was with him that day, for the lines were laden with trout. After taking the fish off the hooks, Hans carefully attached the hare to a hook and threw the line, with its odd catch, back into the stream. Next, he returned to the wood with his load of fish, and placed them in his snares, one by one, just as if they had been caught there.

On reaching home, Hans found Nanette busy about the house, and in the best of spirits. Later, when he asked her to accompany him on his usual round of the snares and fishing lines, she was quite eager to join him.

First the couple proceeded to the river, where Hans said, " I'll see if we have caught anything for supper." Drawing in the lines slowly and steadily, with his wife a most interested spectator, he pulled and pulled, and there, sure enough, was the hare dangling from the hook. Nanette was so astonished that she could only stare, first at the hare, and then at her husband.

" Why do you look so surprised ? " said Hans calmly. " Surely you know that a great many animals can swim, and a few, like the otter and the seal, spend most of their lives in water. Isn't this a lovely water-hare ? " Poor Nanette, quite ignorant of the habits of animals, thought her husband spoke the truth, although she had never heard of such a creature. Putting their catch into a bag, the two continued their walk until they eventually reached the wood.

"Now!" exclaimed Hans, "I wonder if we'll have any luck with the snares ? " If Nanette was surprised to see a hare hooked on a fishing line, she was absolutely amazed to see the fish caught in the traps. But this time she did not show her astonishment, in case her husband would scold her again for her ignorance, and without saying a word, she helped him to release the trout from the snares, and place them in the bag beside the hare.

On the way home they talked and talked as if nothing strange had happened, and when nearing the house Hans said, " Did you hear the news about the Count to-day ? " " No ! What happened ? " replied Nanette eagerly, for she was always keen to listen to the tittle-tattle of the village. " Well," proceeded Hans, " he

burst into the butcher's shop to-day and, in a fit of
temper, threw a leg of mutton at the butcher. However,
the Count soon regretted his hasty action, for the butcher,
chopper in hand, chased his Lordship down the street."
Nanette had been so surprised by the events of the day
that she did not even question the truth of this most
remarkable piece of news.

Three days passed, during which Nanette kept silent
about the treasure, but on the fourth day, when a
neighbour called, she felt that she must tell someone of
her good fortune, and she confided the secret to her
visitor. Needless to say, in a few hours the whole
village had the story of her husband's lucky discovery,
and it became at once the sole topic of conversation
in the district. So quickly did the news spread, that it
reached the ears of the Count that very night. In the
morning, Hans was arrested by two of the Count's
soldiers and taken to the castle to appear before His
Lordship.

When the Count approached Hans he said to him
in a stern voice, " It appears that you have found a
very valuable treasure and have not even troubled to
inform me of your discovery."

" A tr-tr-treasure ? " Hans stammered as if he was bewildered. " A-a treasure ? Do you say that I have found a treasure ? Let me see it, my Lord, for I have much need of it."

" Make no pretence at innocence ! " thundered the Count, " or I shall have you punished. Your wife admits your discovery and she, herself, has told every-one of it."

At the mention of his wife, Hans broke into loud laughter. " My Lord," he said, " Nanette, my wife, is simple, and imagines many stupid notions to be true."

" What ? " replied the Count, " I cannot accept your answer without proof." Turning to two of his guards, he commanded, " Bring this man's wife here immediately ! "

A few minutes later, Nanette stood trembling by the side of her husband. " Tell me," said the Count looking at her severely, " did your husband find a box containing treasure ? " " Yes," replied the frightened woman, " Hans really found a treasure, but he buried it again so that we could use the money later." " How long ago did he find it, my good woman ? " asked the Count. Nanette thought for a moment and said, " Just five days ago. I remember it well, for on the same day, Hans fished a hare out of the river."

The Count looked at her in amazement and Hans interrupted, " You see, my Lord, that I was speaking the truth. I told you she has silly notions." Naturally, this angered Nanette and she turned to her husband and cried, " Notions—indeed ! Why I remember too that you caught several fish in your snares that very same evening."

At these words, even the Count was forced to laugh, and this caused Nanette to lose her temper. "Yes," she declared hotly, "Hans discovered the treasure on the same day that you threw a leg of mutton at the butcher. Surely you can remember the butcher chasing you for your life down the street."

For a few moments the Count stared at her in silence, and then he said quietly to Hans, "Take her home, for in her present state of mind, she could imagine anything."

Shortly afterwards, as the two trudged homewards, Hans said to her, "Well wife! I hope this experience will teach you to keep the next secret I tell you." Although Nanette was too angry to reply, the lesson was not lost upon her, for, from that day, she was more careful of what she told her neighbours.

(Adapted)

INTERESTING FACTS
ABOUT
HOLLAND AND THE DUTCH PEOPLE.

1. Holland, or the Netherlands, is sometimes called " The Land of the Tulip," " The Land of the Hyacinth," " The Land of the Windmill," and the natives of this country are known as the Dutch people.

2. It is a very flat country with scarcely a hill to be seen. In some places the land is much lower than the sea, and the people have constructed sand dunes, and high embankments, and built huge walls or dykes to prevent the water from flooding their farms. Stretches of land which have been reclaimed from sea or river are called **polders**. The word " Holland " means " land of the wood (holt)."

3. The Dutch are fine farmers, and throughout the land may be seen the world famous **bulb farms** of flowers, such as tulips, hyacinths, snowdrops, and daffodils. They are also noted for **cheese-making,**

and export the familiar round red-skinned cheeses about the size and shape of a football.

4. Holland has a great number of **canals**, which provide an important means of communication. On these canals, barges, laden with merchandise, ply their trade between the various towns within Holland, and even cross its borders to go into other European countries. The barge skippers and their families live on board. There are special schools on the main canals, and when the barge is docked for a few days the children attend there. They get homework which they complete before reaching the next school on their route.

5. The whole country is dotted with **windmills**, and they are a special feature of the Dutch landscape. These windmills, which all turn to the left (against the clock), are used to pump the surface water from the fields into the rivers and canals.

6. In the winter, when the waterways are frozen over, these become the playground of the whole nation. Even the Queen goes skating. Everyone takes a holiday, and long-distance skating races are held.

7. Dutch housewives are noted for their cleanliness and thrifty housekeeping. Most families eat a light snack in the middle of the day and have their main meal in the evening. A dish which is very popular with children in Holland is called Hot Lightning. It is made by mashing boiled potatoes and boiled apples together with some bacon dripping and is served, very hot, with the meat course.

8. In the towns, cycling is the favourite method of travel, and the sight of hundreds of cyclists constantly passing to and fro, immediately attracts the stranger's attention. The men seem to be always smoking— either a cigar or a long pipe—and this is no doubt due to the fact that tobacco is very cheap.

9. The Dutch have always been good sailors, and this has helped to make their country prosperous and wealthy. During the seventeenth century, Holland was the world's leading sea-power, and her daring explorers and traders created a large overseas empire in the East and West Indies—an empire which does not exist today. The Netherland Antilles in the West Indies are self-governing though they are part of the Netherlands Realm. Holland still has a very large merchant fleet.

10. About two hundred years ago, independent Dutch farmers settled in South Africa, and cultivated the rich soil of that country. Many British people had settled there, too, and at the end of last century there was a quarrel which led to the Boer War (1899-1902). Now South Africa is an independent country in which the people of Dutch and British descent live together amicably. Afrikaans, the language of the original Dutch pioneers, is still commonly spoken there.

QUESTIONS ON THE STORY.

1. In what country did the story take place?
2. Describe the home of Hans Bloom.
3. How did he obtain a living?
4. What kind of woman was his wife Nanette?
5. What was Hans doing when he discovered the treasure?
6. Name the season of the year.
7. Why was he worried about his newly-found wealth?
8. What did he do with the box containing the treasure?
9. What animal was yoked to the plough?
10. What vow did Nanette make when Hans told her of his wonderful luck?
11. What did Hans do with the trapped hare?
11. What did he do with the fish caught on his lines?
13. Which animals did Hans mention as living most of their lives in water?
14. Relate the story which he told his wife about the Count.
15. For how long did Nanette keep the secret of the treasure?
16. What happened to Hans when the Count heard of his discovery?
17. What excuse did he make for his wife's story?
18. Who brought Nanette before the Count?
19. Why did she completely lose her temper?
20. What advice did the Count give to Hans?

QUESTIONS ON THE INTERESTING FACTS.

1. (a) Give a popular name for Holland.
   (b) What name is given to natives of the country?
2. (a) How is the sea prevented from flooding the land?
   (b) What is the meaning of the word " Holland "?
3. Name two products for which Holland is famous.
4. What would you see in Holland if you went there in late April?
5. How are great quantities of goods transported?
6. What is the purpose of most Dutch windmills?
7. What dish do Dutch children like? How is it made?

8. Holland was once one of the greatest countries in the world. To what was this due?
9. What war broke out between the British and Dutch settlers in South Africa?
10. Name the language of the Dutch settlers in Africa.

DEVELOPMENT EXERCISES.

1. Point out on the map (*a*) Holland, (*b*) The Netherland Antilles, (*c*) South Africa.
2. In Holland, the windmill is used to drain surface water from the fields. For what purpose was the windmill used in Britain? Why was it not a great success? What kind of mill took its place? How is wheat ground into flour nowadays?
3. Hans used an ass to pull his plough. What other creatures are sometimes used for this work? What is the modern method of ploughing?
4. The Dutch are famous flower growers. Name and describe briefly (*a*) four garden flowers, (*b*) four wild flowers.
5. Some animals, like the otter and the seal, spend most of their lives in water. Do you know of any other such animals? Which of them closely resemble fish?
6. The butcher, chopper in hand, chased the Count down the street. Who, in the course of their daily work, use the following: awl, pick, razor, saw, spanner?
7. Snaring is a method of hunting by which the victims are trapped. Which animals are mostly caught by means of traps?
8. In the Netherlands, a great amount of goods is transported on the canals. What is the difference between a river and a canal? Name two world famous canals and point them out on the map.

BAUXITE, THE ALUMINIUM ORE

WHEN you peel the silvery wrapping from a chocolate bar or biscuit you are handling aluminium. Some of the food in the larder is probably wrapped in this kind of aluminium foil which we often call " silver paper." The light silvery-coloured kettle and saucepans on the kitchen shelf are made of this metal too.

Buses have silvery aluminium parts inside, and the outsides of buses are also made of aluminium, though they are covered over by paint. Many buildings have aluminium window frames. And everybody knows that aeroplanes are made of aluminium.

These are only a few uses of this important metal. With all the aluminium about today, it may surprise you to know that it had not been discovered at all until about a hundred years ago, and the process for making it cheaply was not discovered until 1886.

BAUXITE

Lumps of brittle, creamy-white or reddish-brown rock may not seem to have much connection with shining metal, but aluminium, chemically joined with other substances, is contained in a rock known as bauxite. Bauxite takes its name from the French village, Les Baux, where it was discovered by a chemist in the 19th century.

After bauxite rocks have been exposed to the weather for centuries the soluble matter, such as limestone, is washed away, while the aluminium silicates become hard. Heavy rainfall and hot sunshine are the processes of nature which break down the rocks, and the richest deposits of aluminium ore are found in tropical and semi-tropical countries—in Jamaica, Guyana, Ghana, and Queensland in Australia. Although bauxite is found in the more temperate regions of the world also, the deposits there are not of such high quality as those in warm countries.

Jamaica is the world's largest supplier of bauxite, and this product is the island's most important export. It is found there in pockets on the surface of the land, and at depths ranging from ten to one hundred feet, from which it can be obtained by open-pit mining.

BAUXITE MINING

When a deposit is located, engineers make borings to find out its depth, and samples are handed to chemists who analyse them for quality. If the quality is good, and the quantity sufficient to make the deposit worth exploiting, bulldozers are set to work to clear away trees and shrubs. Next, the top soil is removed, and set carefully aside beyond the field of operations. Occasionally, blasting is needed to remove great quantities of earth. Then, giant shovels, capable of holding from two to five tons, take huge bites of the bauxite, and load them into the waiting trucks for transportation in open rail cars. After all the bauxite has been removed from the pit, huge boulders, trees, and other filling material are thrown in, and the whole is levelled off. When the top soil is replaced the land is once more ready for agriculture.

Most of Jamaica's bauxite is exported in its natural state, but some of it is made into alumina before export. The bauxite is crushed and then mixed with chemicals in big steel tanks to get rid of impurities. Alumina is the clean, white powder which is left after this process, and it consists of the metal aluminium tightly joined to the gas, oxygen.

MAKING ALUMINIUM

To separate the alumina from the oxygen electricity is required, and it is to countries which have a plentiful supply of cheap electricity that Jamaica sends bauxite and alumina. Factories for this process are often situated in mountainous regions where dams are built across fast-flowing rivers and the rushing water is made to spin turbine wheels and generate electricity. The electricity is passed through the white powder in such a way that the aluminium is separated from the oxygen, and ingots of aluminium are produced.

The ingots are sent out to factories in big industrial towns to be turned into the right shapes for making the things we need. Sometimes the ingots are melted down and small quantities of other metals are added. The metal is then called an alloy, and it is very strong. The molten metal can be poured into moulds to make very complicated things like the parts for motor engines. Other shapes can be forged by squeezing or hammering lumps of aluminium into dies which have been carved out into the required shapes.

Much of the aluminium is made into flat sheets by being passed to and fro between massive steel rollers.

When a large number of things made from aluminium are wanted, all exactly the same, the sheets are fed into powerful presses which shape the metal. For instance, saucepans are made by feeding circles of sheet aluminium into a press of this kind. Another machine presses out the handles and these are then riveted on.

ALUMINIUM IN THE AIR

One of the wonders of this age is the ease and speed with which we travel immense distances through the air. Aircraft must be fashioned of material which is light and strong, and which can be processed until it is absolutely free from defects. The aluminium industry has served the aircraft industry well, and has played its part in man's conquest of the air. So next time you see a jet liner flashing through the clouds, remember that the making of that silver monster may have started in a bauxite pit in Jamaica.

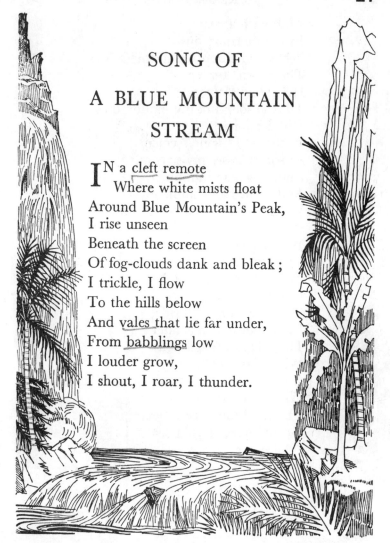

SONG OF
A BLUE MOUNTAIN
STREAM

IN a cleft remote
　Where white mists float
Around Blue Mountain's Peak,
I rise unseen
Beneath the screen
Of fog-clouds dank and bleak;
I trickle, I flow
To the hills below
And vales that lie far under,
From babblings low
I louder grow,
I shout, I roar, I thunder.

I fall with a rush
In the morning hush
While the mountain sleeping lies,
There swift I sleep—
Here slow I creep,
Till the sound of my motion dies:
Oh! I rejoice
In the night wind's voice
As soft it kisses my stream,
And dance and glimmer
And glance and shimmer
Where moonlit reaches gleam.

With ice-cold wave
I gently lave
The flowers as I wander,
I gleam and glide
'Neath Mountain Pride,
I murmur and meander
Thro' Fern-arched dells
Where fairy-bells
And violets scent the air,
While calls above
The soft blue dove
Or lone-voiced Solitaire.

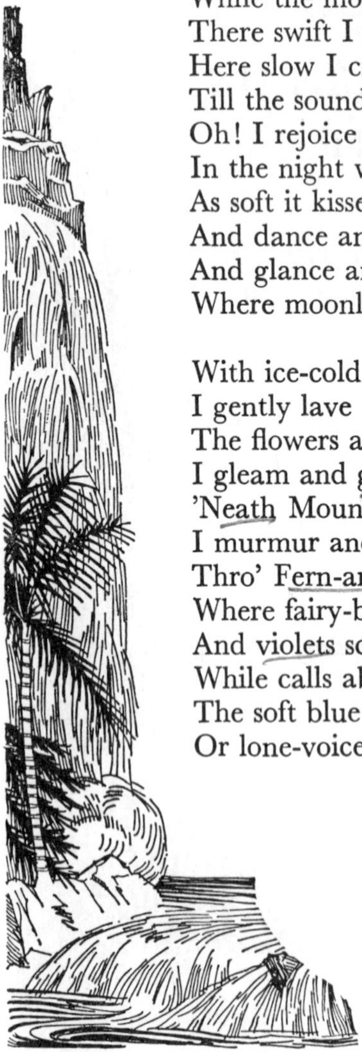

And here I crash
With silver flash
Over a mighty crag,
And the echoes ring
As I headlong fling
The trees I downward drag—
Till last I pour
With deafening roar,
A mountain stream no longer,
O'er plains below,
And seawards flow
A river broad and stronger.

Reginald M. Murray.

THE DISCOVERY OF THE NEW WORLD

ALL through the early ages of history, the East was believed to be a great wonderland, where splendid monarchs ruled over vast and powerful kingdoms. These lands were not only inhabited by strange men, but were also said to contain even stranger flowers, fruits, birds, and animals. Most attractive of all was the legend that gold, silver, and gleaming precious stones could be obtained in abundance, without much difficulty.

The West, on the other hand, was looked upon as a region of danger and mystery, cut off from the rest of the world by fogs, storms, and a never-ending stretch of cold, angry water. In the fifteenth century, however, men began to think and to wonder, and to dream of fresh worlds to conquer, but, strange to say, they only saw in the West, a new gateway to the East.

Among these advanced thinkers was the one who was later to become the most famous explorer of this or any other age—Christopher Columbus. We know very little of his early life, but it is recorded that he was born in Genoa (Italy), served as a navigator in a Genoese ship, and was forced, by Venetian pirates, to seek his livelihood in Portugal.

Columbus believed that the world was round, and he wanted to explore the unknown regions, which lay beyond the Atlantic, because he thought that a straight course due west of Portugal would bring him to the eastern seaboard of Asia—to Zipangu (Japan), the country, which the famous traveller Marco Polo had termed, " The Land of Gold."

The fearless adventurer outlined his plans and sought help in many countries, but without success. After many refusals, he finally won the consent of King Ferdinand and Queen Isabella of Spain, and obtained from them a royal commission giving him authority to take possession of all new lands, and conferring on him the title, " Admiral of the Ocean Sea."

Many difficulties had to be overcome, even after he had received the royal consent ; financial help was hard to get ; ship-owners feared the risks attached to so crazy a voyage ; and crews could not be found, for few men cared to venture out into the unknown sea with no certainty of return. Queen Isabella, however, was so convinced of the sincerity and wisdom of this remarkable sailor, that she provided the necessary money to buy and equip three ships, and instructions were issued that criminals, with seafaring experience, be taken from the gaols to serve as members of the crews. Thus, after repeated setbacks, Columbus was ready to embark on his great adventure, and put all his theories to the test.

On the night of August 2nd, 1492, all was hustle and bustle in the usually quiet little Spanish river-port of Palos. Crowds were moving in the streets, lights were twinkling and torches flaring, as the church bell boomed out a solemn toll, summoning the people to take part in a farewell service for those who were to set out in a few hours on the greatest voyage in history.

Inside the church, the crews and captains of the three ships were grouped around the leader of the expedition. After they had received the blessing of the Church upon their venture and the service was over, the crews, headed by their Admiral and captains, marched down the cobbled streets to the harbour. The crowd streamed along with them, shouting farewells and words of encouragement and good cheer.

Once on board, the sailors immediately set to making their ships ready for departure. About day-break, when all the necessary preparations had been completed, the anchors were raised and the vessels moved towards the open sea. The Admiral's flagship, the " Santa

Maria," a great red cross on her main-sail and the royal standard of Spain aloft, led the way, while following close astern were the " Pinta," and the " Nina." And so these little ships—tiny ships when compared with the huge liners of modern times—sailed away to face the perils of unknown and uncharted seas.

Trouble began when they reached the Canary Islands, as the volcano at Teneriffe was in eruption, and the crews were afraid of the awe-inspiring sight. It must be remembered that at this time people were very easily frightened, as they believed in witches, demons, and all the spectres of the Dark Ages. Matters became worse, when these isles had disappeared behind them, and they were alone in the wide Atlantic. Some of the sailors protested to their captains that they were challenging the wrath of Heaven, and foretold that they would come to a horrible and untimely death. Columbus, however, assured them that they were perfectly safe so long as they continued to obey his orders, and he promised them large and rich rewards, when they reached " The Land of Gold."

For seven weeks, the little fleet held on its westward course, and happily met with smooth seas and favourable winds. The courage of Columbus never wavered, but, on the other hand, the fears of his men increased as day followed day without any sight of land. Some of them declared that they were being led by a madman, who was prepared to sacrifice all their lives in a hopeless effort to prove his absurd, fantastic notions.

So alarmed and disgruntled were the sailors that there were even rumblings of mutiny, and the

situation became tense and serious. The Admiral, however, was equal to the occasion, and proved himself a
capable leader. He renewed his promises of rich reward
to the greedy, threatened the cowards with punishment,
and told them that, unless they sighted land in another
week, the ships would swing about and sail for home.

Columbus calculated the total distance they had
already travelled, and reckoned that his fleet should
be off the coast of Japan. He set a sharp look-out
on the western horizon, and two days later—on a
bright October morning—that, which they all had
hoped and prayed for, came in view. There were
frantic cries of " Land ahead ! " The sailors were
beside themselves with joy. The explorer could
hardly contain himself as he realised that all his dreams
had come true, and that his great adventure had been
crowned with success.

The land which they had sighted was an inhabited island, and Columbus ordered the small boats to be got ready, so that they could go ashore and ascertain their exact whereabouts. The Admiral landed at a little cove, and, after the royal standard of Spain had been planted on a hillock, claimed possession of the island on behalf of King Ferdinand and Queen Isabella.

Around the landing party there soon gathered a crowd of dark-skinned natives, who had crept out of their hiding-places to gaze in wonderment and awe at the strangers. They were very friendly to their white visitors, and brought them gifts of fruit and bread. The natives were delighted to receive in exchange such things as coloured beads, and cheap metal trinkets.

Now Columbus did not know that he was near America, but thought he had discovered a new island near Japan. The explorer called the island, San Salvador (now known as Watling Island), and, as he judged the natives to be of a race which peopled India, he called them Indians. Ever since then, the group of islands hereabouts has been known as the West Indies, in order to distinguish them from the East Indies— half the world away.

All three crews had been eagerly expecting to come to a land where rich treasure was to be found, and the thought of untold wealth filled their minds with greed. Noticing that some of the people wore valuable necklets and bracelets, the sailors asked them, by means of signs, whence the gold had come. The natives replied by pointing to the South, and they indicated to the voyagers that gold, silver, and precious stones could be obtained there.

Next day, the ships set sail in quest of the lands to which they had been directed, and thus the islands of Cuba and Haiti were discovered. Gold and silver articles were in common use among the natives there, and many of the heavy and valuable ornaments were taken aboard the ships. At Haiti, the " Santa Maria " was wrecked on a sandbar, and from her timbers, Columbus built a fort for a few members of the crew, who had decided to settle there and become the first colony of the new world. The explorer, now aboard the " Nina," decided to sail for Spain and, accompanied by the " Pinta," the vessels were soon homeward bound. After a rough and stormy crossing, they reached their starting point, the little river-port of Palos.

Columbus received a splendid welcome, and was acclaimed and honoured at the Spanish Court. The people flocked to see the many wonders he had brought back, and they marvelled greatly at the strange plants, and birds, and, most of all, at the six dark-skinned natives who had come with him. The explorer soon became a national hero, and was fêted throughout the country.

Naturally the Spaniards fitted out many expeditions so that they could reap the benefit of these rich possessions as soon as possible. Columbus made several more voyages to the West, and discovered the islands of Dominica, Santa Cruz, Trinidad, and the mainland of South America. He established new colonies, and much of the great wealth of the natives was shipped to Spain, which soon became the richest country in the world.

Many adventurers of the worst type flocked to the new colonies, and the story of their get-rich-quick methods is a terrible tale of native oppression and slavery. Columbus protested, and consequently fell into bad grace, as the colonists were interested only in amassing as much wealth as they could. Even King Ferdinand forsook the gallant explorer, who died some years later in poverty and neglect.

And so America (named after a later explorer—Amerigo Vespucci) was discovered by Christopher Columbus. At that time, it was not known to be a great new continent, and not until after his death was it realised that he had added a New World to the Old.

(Adapted.)

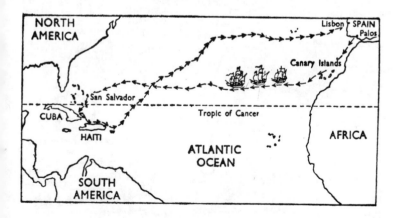

NORTH POLE

PEARY
1909

VIKINGS

JOHN and SEBASTIAN
CABOT 1497

CHRISTOPHER
COLUMBUS
1492

MUNGO PARK
1796

BARTHOLOMEW DIAZ
1486

N
W E
S

FERDINAND MAGELLAN
1521

ROALD
AMUNDSEN
1911

SOUTH POLE

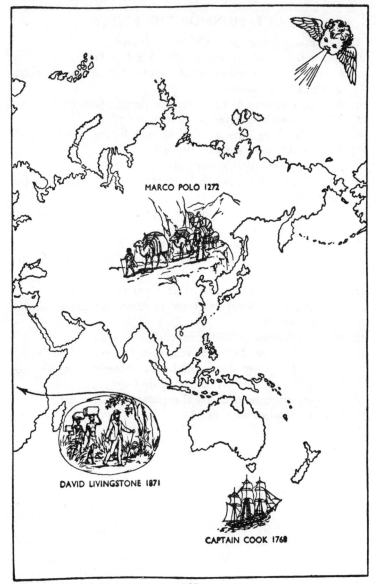

MARCO POLO 1272

DAVID LIVINGSTONE 1871

CAPTAIN COOK 1768

QUESTIONS ON THE STORY.

1. Where was Christopher Columbus born ?
2. How did he come to seek his livelihood in Portugal ?
3. According to Columbus, what country lay on the other side of the Atlantic Ocean ?
4. Who gave consent and help for his daring adventure ?
5. What title was conferred on him ?
6. Name the three ships which took part in the expedition.
7. From which port did they leave ?
8. In what year did they set sail ?
9. What caused the crews to be frightened when they reached the Canary Islands ?
10. What kind of weather did the expedition experience on the westward voyage ?
11. Why did the sailors threaten to mutiny ?
12. What name did Columbus give to the first island he discovered ?
13. How did the natives treat their unexpected visitors ?
14. Why did the adventurers leave to search for islands further to the South ?
15. What misfortune befell the expedition at Haiti ?
16. How was the explorer received when he returned to Spain ?
17. Name other places discovered by Columbus in later voyages.
18. How did these colonies benefit Spain ?
19. In what circumstances did the gallant explorer die ?
20. Why is America so called ?

QUESTIONS ON THE MAP OF EXPLORATION.

1. Who first reached the North Pole ?
2. Who first reached the South Pole ?
3. Name two famous explorers of Africa.
4. Who were said to have visited Greenland in early times ?
5. Who first discovered America ?
6. Who first rounded South America and sailed from the Atlantic into the Pacific ?
7. Who first rounded the Cape of Good Hope at the southern tip of Africa ?
8. What famous traveller explored and returned with wonderful tales of the Far East ?
9. What famous English navigator explored and charted New Zealand and Eastern Australia ?
10. Who are credited with the discovery of Canada ?

KINDNESS REWARDED

LONG ago, in the land of Greece, there was a town in which the people had become very hard-hearted and wicked. Whenever strangers entered its streets, instead of welcoming them with kind words of greeting and offering a temporary resting-place, these rude people closed their doors to wayfarers, and even pelted them with mud and stones. The children, having been set this bad example by their parents, would follow the travellers through the streets, and jeer, shout, make ugly faces, and encourage their dogs to attack the leg-weary wanderers.

Far and wide, the place became notorious for its lack of hospitality. 'Tis strange yet true that in olden times the virtue of hospitality was more thought of than nowadays, and thus the evil customs and conduct of these wicked people were considered all the more shocking.

On the outskirts of the town there stood a modest little cottage thatched with straw, and in it dwelt an old couple, Philemon and his wife Baucis. These old folk were quite poor, but, in spite of their poverty, they were contented and happy, and always showed kindness to strangers. Old Philemon toiled in his garden, while Baucis kept the cottage as clean as a new pin. They lived chiefly on bread, milk, vegetables, honey from their beehive, and grapes from the vine which grew against the cottage wall.

One evening, two travel-stained strangers entered the gates of the town. One was a tall, noble-looking man of athletic build and fine features. His companion was of slight build and much younger, and there was something unusually bright and quick about him. Indeed, so light was he, that at times his feet hardly seemed to touch the ground. He wore a curious cap, and in his left hand he carried a staff, which was made of olive wood, and had something like a pair of wings near the top. Two small snakes, carved in the wood, were entwined about the staff and looked very life-like.

The travellers knocked at several doors and asked for a night's shelter, but at every house they were refused and received harsh words in answer to their request. As usual, a crowd of children soon gathered, and followed the tired wanderers with loud hoots and cries. Philemon and Baucis had already eaten their frugal supper, when they heard the loud shouts of the children, and the angry barking of dogs. Both went immediately to the door, and when they saw the strangers approaching, hastened to meet them.

" Friends," said old Philemon, " our cottage is small, and our fare humble, but we shall be honoured if you will share it with us. Pay no attention to these rude children, and we will try to make amends for the unkindness of our neighbours." The strangers gladly accepted the invitation, and were soon seated by the hearth, while Philemon heaped logs on the fire and Baucis prepared a simple meal.

As both strangers kept filling and refilling their glasses with milk, Baucis became quite worried, for she knew the pitcher must soon be emptied, and there was not another drop of milk in the house. Imagine her surprise when, peeping into the pitcher, she saw that it was full to the brim, and that every time they emptied the vessel, it refilled itself. Baucis was struck dumb with wonder, but when she recovered from her amazement, she whispered to her husband what she had seen. The old couple then watched more closely, and they noticed that the honey had a richer, golden colour and sweeter scent, and that the little bunches of green grapes from the stunted vine in the garden had become much bigger, and had changed to purple-black clusters.

Although they were astonished at all they saw, both husband and wife did not speak of the wonders they had witnessed, but continued waiting on their guests. At last, saying that they had thoroughly enjoyed their supper, the visitors rose from the table and asked if they could obtain a place in which to sleep, for they had walked a great distance that day, and were very tired. Baucis then showed her guests to the little bedroom, and bade them good-night. When she returned, the good old folk discussed the wonderful events of the evening, and later both lay down on the kitchen floor and fell fast asleep.

Next morning, the old man and his wife rose early, but before Baucis could prepare breakfast, the two guests appeared and, after thanking her for all her kindness, begged to be excused for not waiting, as they had a long day's journey ahead of them. The elder of the two guests asked the old couple to accompany them a little way, in order to direct them on their road. When they reached the top of a nearby hill, all turned to have a view of the town—and at the sight which met their gaze, Philemon and Baucis trembled in awe-struck silence. Where, a few moments before, had stood row upon row of houses, there was now a lake sparkling in the morning sunlight, and no sign of their wicked neighbours or their dwellings could be seen. Most wonderful of all, in place of their own little thatched cottage was a magnificent palace of shining marble.

Jupiter, the taller of the two strangers, turned with a smile to the astonished couple. " My good friends," he said, " these people were hard-hearted and wicked. They had none of the virtues which make this a happier and better world, and it is perhaps fitting that the lake should spread itself, as of old, above the site of their dwellings. You, on the other hand, have shown such kindness, without hope of reward, that your bread and milk became the food and drink of the gods. To show our sincere appreciation of all that you have done for us, ask any favour you choose, and it shall be granted."

Philemon looked at his wife for a moment or two, and in a trembling voice said, " Our dearest wish is to live together while we live, and to die together when we pass from this world, so that neither of us may mourn the loss of the other. If it please you to grant this request, my good wife and I would be very, very happy."

" Be it so ! Your wish is granted," said Jupiter. " Live in the temple which now takes the place of your humble abode. Act as the guardians of the palace, and show your customary kindness to all strangers who pass this way."

No sooner were these words spoken than he and his companion Mercury vanished from sight, and the old couple were left alone on the highway. Both slowly retraced their steps, discussing excitedly the recent amazing turn of events, and fearing each moment that it was all a trick of the imagination.

For many years Philemon and Baucis lived in the palace, and nothing gave them greater happiness than to give good cheer to travellers who passed that way. Whenever strangers came to the temple, they were gladly welcomed and kindly entertained, for, though they now lived in such rich surroundings, the husband and wife were just as simple and kind as they had been in their poverty.

One day the kind, old couple were missed by their guests, and despite a frantic search everywhere, they could not be found. It was noticed, however, that in front of the palace stood two stately, majestic trees— one, an oak tree, and the other, a linden tree. Strange to relate, the visitors could not remember having seen these particular trees there on the day before.

No trace was ever found of Philemon and Baucis, and so it must be taken for granted that their dearest wish had been fulfilled. Many people, who later chanced to pass that way, heard the story of this kind old couple, and some would hang garlands of flowers on the branches of the two trees, and sit beneath their shade, listening to the wind murmuring among the leaves.

*Adapted from " Legends of Greece and Rome," by
Grace H. Kupfer.*

INTERESTING FACTS
ABOUT
GREECE AND THE GREEKS.

1. The ancient Greeks called their own country "Hellas" and themselves "**Hellenes**," names in use to the present day. The land was very rough and mountainous, and there were no good roads from one part of the country to another. Most of the towns were built round an **acropolis** or hill, to which the people went in time of danger.

2. In olden times, the country we now know as Greece was made up of city-states—each completely separate and having its own government, laws and customs. The greatest city-states were **Athens** and **Sparta** : prominent also, were **Corinth** and **Thebes**.

3. (*a*) In Athens, a child was named on the tenth day according to custom. When a boy, of well-to-do parents, reached seven years of age, he was placed in the care of a **pedagogue** or personal attendant, who was generally a slave. The pedagogue accompanied the boy to and from school, and acted as his guardian. (*b*) From early childhood, the Spartans trained themselves to become soldiers, and their state was like a military camp. Slaves did all the household work, and this left the citizens free for their hard, strict training.

4. The houses were made of sun-dried bricks and had flat roofs. A host and his guests reclined on couches, during friendly visits. The door-knocker was usually a ring in a lion's mouth and was said to keep away evil. Inlaid in the entrance passage was the Greek word for " Welcome," and this is probably the origin of the same salute on the modern door-mat. The Athenians were very early risers, and thought nothing of calling on their friends, shortly after sunrise.

5. The men, accompanied by their slaves who acted as carriers, went to the market-places to make household purchases. Their food consisted chiefly of barley porridge with salt or honey, dried salted fish, and barley cakes and loaves. Apples were rare, and considered a valuable delicacy. The barber's shop was very popular, for there they heard the latest news, true or otherwise, from the slave who trimmed their hair or beard.

6. The men wore either a sleeveless tunic or a long mantle, the latter being worn on special occasions.

The women wore a long, loosely-draped mantle with a girdle. Sandals were the common footwear.

7. At one time Athens was noted for its many temples, buildings, and statues, and was regarded as the most beautiful city in the world. The **Parthenon**, most famous of all Greek buildings, contained the city's protecting goddess **Athene** (pronounced A-theen'-ay). All the public holidays were connected with religion, and the songs, dances, processions, and plays were held in honour of some god or goddess.

8. The Greeks were very fond of music, plays, and all kinds of physical exercises. The famous Games at **Olympia** took place every four years and consisted of running, jumping, wrestling, and chariot race competitions. The winner of each event was rewarded with an olive wreath, which was considered the highest honour in sport.

9. One old Greek method of telling the time was by measuring the shadow of a stick, which was stuck in the ground. Instead of asking a guest to come for dinner at six o'clock (as we do nowadays), he would be invited to dine at ten feet of the shadow. One could never escape the chirping of crickets in Athens, and the people liked them so much that they had designs of this creature on their buckles and brooches.

10. At one time Athens was the centre of world learning. The great Greek philosophers **Socrates, Plato**, and **Aristotle** tried to lead the people to a discovery of truth by their clever, clear thinking in conversation. **Euclid** wrote a book on **Geometry**, which is the study of figures such as triangles, squares, and circles. **Aesop**, a Greek slave, was a famous story-teller, who made the animals talk and act so cleverly in his fables that they are widely-read and popular to this day.

QUESTIONS ON THE STORY.

1. In what country did this story take place ?
2. What kind of people lived in the town ?
3. Who followed their bad example ?
4. Where did Philemon and Baucis stay ?
5. What big word is used in the story for " kindness to strangers " ?
6. Complete the following sentence. The old couple lived chiefly on ——————————.
7. Describe the two strangers.
8. How did the children misbehave ?
9. How did the old couple receive the weary travellers ?
10. What simple meal did Baucis prepare for her unexpected guests ?
11. Why were the old folks struck dumb with wonder during the supper ?
12. Where did Philemon and Baucis sleep that night ?
13. What excuse did the strangers give for not waiting to breakfast ?
14. When departing, what did the elder of the visitors ask them to do ?
15. What had become of (a) the town, (b) the cottage ?
16. Give the names of the two strangers.
17. What was the old couple's dearest wish ?
18. After granting their request, what instructions did the gods give them ?
19. What appeared in the garden on the day that the old couple vanished ?
20. What did many of the passers-by do when they heard the story of Philemon and Baucis ?

QUESTIONS ON THE INTERESTING FACTS.

1. What do the Greeks call their country ?

2. Name three of the great city-states of ancient Greece ?
3. What was the name given to the personal attendant of a boy at school ?
4. Describe a form of Greek door-knocker.
5. Greek food consisted chiefly of ——————————.
6. Describe the garments worn by the ancient Greeks.
7. What is the most famous of all Greek buildings ?
8. (a) How often did the Olympic Games take place ?
   (b) What award was considered the highest honour at these sports ?
9. Give an old Greek method of telling the time.
10. Name two famous Greek philosophers.

DEVELOPMENT EXERCISES.

1. Point out Greece on the map. In what part of Europe is it ?
2. Hospitality is a virtue. Can you name any other virtues or good qualities which people may possess ?
3. The villagers, old and young, were very ill-mannered. In what ways could they have shown good manners to strangers ?
4. In modern villages and towns there are special houses in which food and shelter can be obtained for payment. What are these guest-homes called ? By whom are they used ?
5. The old couple grew vegetables in their small garden. Name three kinds of vegetables which are usually grown in (a) small gardens, (b) large fields.
6. The men, accompanied by slaves who acted as carriers, bought the household food in the market place. Who buys your food ? How is it brought to the house ? From whom do you get (a) meat, (b) bread, (c) fish, (d) milk, (e) general foodstuffs ?
7. Athens was noted for its many large and beautiful buildings. What are the finest buildings in your village, town, or city ? What is the most beautiful building you have ever seen ?
8. An old Greek method of telling the time was by measuring the shadow of a stick. Do you know of any other methods, ancient or modern, of measuring time ?

A BUSY MORNING

ONE fine morning Jack discovered, on the other side of the hedge, an apple tree bearing tempting fruit ; and he immediately broke through the hedge, and, climbing the tree, he plucked the fairest of the apples, and did eat.

" I say, you, sir. What are you doing there ? " said a rough voice. Jack looked down and saw a stout, thick-set person, in a grey coat and red waistcoat, standing underneath him.

" I'm eating apples," replied Jack. " Shall I throw you down a few ? "

" Thank you kindly. The fewer that are pulled the better. Those apples are mine, and I'll trouble you to come down as fast as you please. When you're down, we can settle our accounts," continued the man, shaking his stick. " I've lost plenty of apples and have long wanted to find out the robbers. Now I've caught one, I'll take good care he doesn't escape without apple sauce. So come down, you young thief, come down directly, or it will be the worse for you."

" Thank you," said Jack, " but I am very well here. I will, if you please, argue the point from where I am."

"I've no time to argue the point, my lad. I've plenty to do, but don't think I'll let you off. If you don't choose to come down, why then, you may stay there, and I'll answer for it, as soon as my work is done I'll find you safe enough."

"He'll not find me here when he comes back, I've a notion," thought Jack. But in this Jack was mistaken. The farmer walked to the hedge, and called to a boy, who took his orders and ran to the farmhouse. In a minute or two, a large bulldog was seen bounding along the orchard to his master.

"Mark him, Caesar," said the farmer to the dog. "Mark him." The dog crouched down in the grass, with his head up, and eyes glaring at Jack. "I can't wait here. But Caesar can, and I'll tell you as a friend,

that if he gets hold of you, he'll not leave a limb of you together. When work's done, I'll come back." So saying, the farmer walked off, leaving Jack and the dog to argue the point, if they felt like doing so.

After a while, the dog laid his head down and closed his eyes as if asleep. But Jack observed that at the least movement on his part, one eye was seen to unclose partly. So Jack, like a prudent boy, resolved to stay where he was. He picked a few more apples, for it was his dinner time, and as he chewed he thought.

Jack had been but a few minutes thinking and chewing when he was interrupted by another chewing animal, nothing less than a bull, which had been turned out with full possession of the orchard, and now advanced, bellowing occasionally, and tossing his head at the sight of Caesar, which he considered to be as much a trespasser as his master had considered our hero.

Caesar started up and faced the bull, which advanced pawing, with its tail in the air. When within a few yards the bull made a rush at the dog, which avoided it and attacked it in turn.

Thus did the warfare continue until the two animals were at some distance from the apple tree. Jack prepared for immediate flight, but unfortunately the combat was carried on by the side of the hedge at which Jack had made his way in. " Never mind," thought Jack. " There are two sides to every field. At all events I'll try it."

He was slipping down the trunk when he heard a tremendous roar. The bulldog had been tossed by the bull. He was then high in the air, and Jack saw him

fall on the other side of the hedge.   Upon this, Jack,
seeing that he was relieved from his sentry, slipped down
the rest of the tree and took to his heels.

Unfortunately for Jack, the bull saw him, and,
flushed with victory, immediately set up another roar
and bounded after him. Jack saw his danger, and fear
gave him wings. Not only did he fly over the orchard :
he flew over the hedge, which was about five feet high,
just as the bull drove its head into it.

" Look before you leap " is an old proverb.   Had
Jack done so he would have fared better. But as there
were very good reasons why he didn't look, we will
excuse him. We will merely state that when Jack got
to the other side of the hedge, he found he had pitched
upon two beehives and upset them. The bees were not
pleased with Jack for disturbing them, and he had hardly

time to get to his feet before he found them very busily stinging him in all parts. All that he could do was to run for it.

But the bees flew faster than he could run, and he was mad with pain when he stumbled, half-blinded, over the brickwork of a well. He could not stop himself, but he seized the iron chain as it struck him in the face. Down he went, and round went the windlass, and after a rapid descent of fifty feet, our hero found himself under water, and no longer troubled with the bees.

Jack rose from the water and seized the rope to which the chain of the bucket was made fast—it had all been unwound from the windlass and enabled him to keep his head above the surface. After a few seconds he felt something against his legs. It was the bucket, about two feet under water. He put his feet into it and found himself fairly comfortable ; for the water, after the sting of the bees and the heat he had been put into by the bees, was quite cool and refreshing.

" At all events," thought Jack, " if it had not been for the bull I should have been watched by the dog and then thrashed by the farmer. But then again, if it had not been for the bull, I should not have tumbled among the bees. And if it had not been for the bees, I should not have tumbled down the well. But if it had not been for the chain, I should have been drowned."

" However, I've got rid of the farmer, and the dog, and the bull, and the bees. But how am I to get out of this well ? "

After he had been there about fifteen minutes, his teeth began to chatter and his limbs to tremble. He felt numb all over. At first he did not call for help because he was afraid of being pulled up to encounter the farmer. But he was just thinking of shouting when he felt the chain being pulled up, and he slowly emerged from the water. Then he heard complaints about the weight of the bucket, at which he was not surprised. At last his head appeared above the low wall, and he was just about to take hold of it when those who were working the windlass beheld him. It was a farm-hand and a maidservant.

" Thank you," said Jack.

The girl screamed and let go. The man also was startled and did not hold fast. The handle slipped from his grasp, whirled round, struck him under the chin, and threw him headlong before the " Thank you " was fairly out of Jack's lips.

Down like lightning went Jack again to the bottom. Fortunately for him he had not let go the chain ; otherwise he might have struck the sides and been killed. As it was he was merely soused a second time, and in a minute or two was back again in his former position. " This is mighty pleasant," thought Jack, " but, at any rate, they know that I'm here."

Meanwhile the girl ran into the kitchen and fell on the floor in a faint and rolled on some heaps of dough which were laid there before the fire.

"Mercy on me, what's the matter with Susan ? " exclaimed the farmer's wife. " Where's Mary ? Where's John ? "

John soon followed, holding his under-jaw in his hand. He looked very dismal, because he thought his jaw was broken, and he looked very frightened, because he thought he had seen the Devil.

" Mercy on us, what's the matter ? " exclaimed the farmer's wife again. " Mary, Mary, Mary ! " screamed she, beginning to be frightened herself ; for with all her efforts she could not move Susan off her bed of dough, where she lay in a swoon.

Mary answered her mistress's loud appeal, and together they raised Susan (but as for the bread, it never rose again).

" Why don't you come and help, John ? " cried Mary.

" Aw-yaw-aw ! " remarked John, holding his jaw.

" What's the matter here, missus ? " exclaimed the farmer, coming in. " Hoighty-toity, what ails Susan ? And what ails you, John ? Bless me ! Everything seems to go wrong to-day. First, there be the apples stolen. Then there be the bees turned topsy-turvy in the garden. Then there be Caesar with his flank opened by the bull. Then there be the bull broken through the hedge and tumbled into the sand-pit. And now, when I come to get more help to drag him out, I find Susan dead-like, and John looks as if he had seen a ghost."

" Aw-yaw-aw ! " replied John, nodding his head.

At this moment Susan opened her eyes, and came to her senses. " Oh, oh, ma'am ! the well, the well ! " she cried.

" The well ? " said the farmer. " Something wrong there, I suppose. Well, I'll go and see."

The farmer trotted off to the well. He saw the bucket

was at the bottom and all the rope out. He looked about him, and then he looked into the well.

" Here I am," cried Jack. " Get me up quick, or I shall be dead." What he said was true. He was quite done up with being down so long, although his courage had not failed him.

" Confound it, but there be somebody fallen into the well," cried the farmer ; " no end to mishaps this day. Well, we must get a Christian out of a well before we get a bull out of a sand-pit, so I'll go and call the men."

In a very short time, the men at the sand-pit were brought to the well.

" Down there below, hold on now ! " cried the farmer.

" Never fear," answered Jack.

Round went the handle and soon Jack could see about him again. As soon as he was at the top, the men hauled him over the bricks and laid him on the grass, for his strength had failed him.

" Mercy on us, if it bain't the chap who was on my apple tree ! " cried the farmer. " However, he mustn't die for stealing apples. Lift him up, lads, and take him in. He's dead with cold, and no wonder." The farmer led the way, and the men carried Jack into the house, where he was given a hot drink, and in a short time was all right again.

After Jack had told the farmer all that had happened, the latter inquired, " What may be your name? "

" My name is Easy," replied Jack.

" What ! Be you the son of Mr. Easy, of Forest Hill? " exclaimed the farmer.

" Yes," said Jack.

" Hang it, he be my landlord, and a right good landlord, too. Why didn't you say so when you were up in the apple tree? You might have picked the whole orchard, and welcome," said the farmer.

From " Mr. Midshipman Easy," by Captain Marryatt.

INTERESTING FACTS
ABOUT
BRITISH AND CARIBBEAN CROPS

1. Everyone must eat in order to live, and therefore it is essential that plenty of good and proper food should be easily obtainable. On **Farms**, various kinds of food are produced and as these foods are necessary to maintain our health and strength, the farmer's work is of prime importance.

2. There are many different types of farms, such as (*a*) **Arable** farms (growing crops), (*b*) **Dairy** farms (milking cows), (*c*) **Live-stock** farms (grazing cattle and sheep), (*d*) **Hill** farms (grazing sheep), (*e*) **Fruit** farms (growing fruit), and (*f*) **Poultry** farms (rearing egg-laying birds). Generally speaking, however, most farmers grow a variety of grain and vegetable crops and also rear cattle, sheep, pigs, and hens.

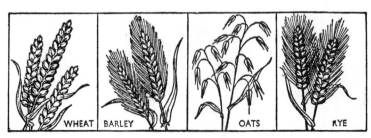

WHEAT   BARLEY   OATS   RYE

3. (*a*) The common British **grain crops** are wheat, barley, and oats.

- (1) **Wheat** is sent to the miller, who grinds it into the white-powdered flour which is made into bread.
- (2) **Barley** is used as a cereal in soups, and also in making malt for whisky.
- (3) **Oats** are used to make oatmeal for bannocks and porridge, and also to feed horses and cattle.

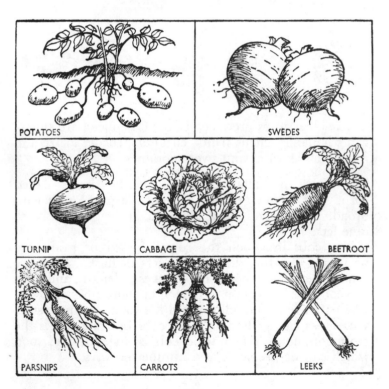

POTATOES

SWEDES

TURNIP

CABBAGE

BEETROOT

PARSNIPS

CARROTS

LEEKS

(*b*) The common farm-grown **vegetables** are potatoes, swedes, turnips, cabbages, beetroot, parsnips, carrots, and leeks. All are important because of their high food value.

4. The seeds of wheat, oats and barley are generally sown early in the year.

—In spring, the seeds sprout green shoots.

—In summer, the shoots grow and gradually turn from green to yellow.

—In autumn, the grain ripens and becomes golden-brown in colour.

The chief crops produced in the Caribbean are **sugarcane, bananas, citrus fruits, coconuts, cocoa, maize** and roots such as yams and sweet potatoes.

5. Maize or Indian corn is generally simply called corn. It is a quick-growing plant of the grass family with broad, long leaves, and grows to a height of six to nine feet.

The cobs in which the rows of seed or grain are borne are sheathed in many layers of husk. They are usually between five and nine inches in length, and each cob contains from eight to sixteen or more rows of grain. The cobs are borne midway up the stalk. A single stalk sometimes carries two or more cobs but one cob is the most common. The unripe cob is an article of food which can be prepared in a number of ways.

6. Bananas thrive best in a hot, moist atmosphere. The banana farmer digs well down into loamy soil, and plants the banana suckers about eighteen inches deep. The suckers are set at an angle of 45°. The plants need a lot of water, but care must be taken to ensure that moisture does not collect round the roots. It takes at least six weeks for the plants to settle down and make new growth; then the plants are pruned or cut back to make them sturdy.

7. Sugar-cane can be grown wherever the climate is warm and there is a good supply of water. The tops or cuttings are planted by hand, at different angles, and in about a week these begin to sprout. About a month after planting all the buds should show signs of growth. Sugar-cane needs lots of water if it is to grow well, and more than half of the crops in the Caribbean have to be irrigated. It is ten to fourteen months before the sugar-cane is ready for harvesting.

8. Coconut trees grow best in a loamy soil which allows water to drain away from the roots. For that reason the finest groves are found on the sea-coast. The dry, unhusked nuts are planted on their sides in nursery beds, and take about three months to sprout. Six months after planting, when the shoots are about nine inches tall, the seedlings, with nuts attached, are transplanted. At this stage it is important to protect the young trees from drought. At harvest time the nuts should be picked regularly every two months.

9. The chief **citrus fruits** grown in the Caribbean are oranges, grapefruits and hybrids such as the ortanique and ugli. These fruits flourish in well-drained, loamy soil, and the groves or orchards must be manured

at regular intervals. Citrus is an important export, and great care is needed in harvesting and packing the fruit so that it arrives overseas in good condition. The fruit should not be gathered in the early morning when it is easily damaged.

10. Yams are portions of underground stems known as tubers. The upper portion of the yam plant is a climbing vine which dies after each growing season. The tuber stores up food and other materials to start growth for the following season. Only a part of the tuber is used for planting as the greater part is used for food. These parts are called " sets " or " heads," and are usually taken from that part of the tuber from which the vine springs. In some varieties whole yams are cut up in bits for planting.

Yam tubers are generally reaped whole at the time when the vines begin to turn yellow and die; " heads " are cut off and allowed to cure in readiness for planting. The " heads " are then allowed to sprout. The sprouting is best done in a cool, dark place, and the method is to spread them out under a shade and cover them with trash.

Yams require good soil and proper tillage. The land in which they are to be planted must be ploughed or forked and be worked into hills or into continuous banks of earth.

QUESTIONS ON THE STORY

1. What was the boy's Christian name?

2. What was he doing in the tree?

3. Describe the farmer.

4. What was the dog's name?

5. What kind of dog was he?

6. What other animal decided to take full possession of the orchard?

7. How did the unequal combat between the two creatures end?

8. What did Jack do when he was relieved of his sentry?

9. How was the lad most unfortunate in his escape from the orchard?

10. What punishment did the angry insects inflict upon the intruder?

11. What accident helped him to escape their unwelcome attention?

12. How did he keep from drowning?

13. Why did he not call for help?

14. Who received a shock when they saw him appear out of the well?

15. Why was the farmer's wife frightened by Susan, the milk-maid?

16. Who came to the assistance of the farmer's wife?

17. Describe how Jack was eventually rescued from the well.

18. What was Jack's surname?

19. Why was the farmer greatly surprised when he heard the boy's name?

20. From the farmer's point of view, give in order, the unusual events of the morning.

QUESTIONS ON THE INTERESTING FACTS

1. Why is the farmer's work very important?

2. Name five different types of farms in Britain.

3. Name the chief crops of the Caribbean.

4. Describe maize when it is ready for harvesting.

5. How does the banana farmer plant suckers?

6. (a) Tell how sugar-cane is planted.
   (b) What do the canes need to make them grow well?

7. (a) Where are the finest coconut groves usually found? Why?
   (b) Explain how new groves are started.

8. What conditions are needed for good citrus crops?

9. How do we know when yams are ready for reaping?

10. How are the yam " heads " prepared before planting?

DEVELOPMENT EXERCISES

1. Apples grow on trees.
   Name (*a*) three fruits which grow on trees.
         (*b*) three fruits which grow on bushes.
2. Caesar was the farmer's bulldog.
   What other kinds of dogs can be useful around a farm ?
   What helpful work could they do ?
3. Complete the following :—

bull	cow	calf
stallion	————	————
boar	————	————
cock	————	————
drake	————	————
gander	————	————

4. Explain the difference between :—
   hay — straw, ham — bacon, spade — shovel, pond — lake.
5. Wheat, barley, and oats are important British grain crops.
   Name other cereals which are grown for food.
6. Name the homes of the following creatures —*e.g.* horse—
   stable.
     Cow, pig, hen, dog, bee.
7. The flesh of the cow is termed **beef**.
   What is the name given to the flesh of the :—sheep, lamb,
   calf, pig, deer ?
8. On a recent visit to a farm I heard various animal sounds.
   I heard a cock——, a cow——, a horse———, a pig——,
   a duck——, a lamb——, and a dog——.

*(The following extract is taken from " TOM SAWYER "
—a story which relates the many everyday adventures of
an American boy. This very popular yarn was written
by the famous humorist, Samuel L. Clemens, who used
the pen-name of " Mark Twain.")*

THE ADVENTURES OF
TOM SAWYER

" Tom! "
No answer.
" Tom! "
No answer.
" Where is that boy, I wonder ? You, Tom! "
The old lady pulled her spectacles down and looked
over them about the room ; then she put them up and
looked out under them. She looked perplexed for a
moment, and then said, not fiercely, but still loud
enough for the furniture to hear :—
" Well, if I get hold of you, I'll—— "
She did not finish, for by this time she was bending
down and punching under the bed with the broom,
and so she needed breath to punctuate the punches with.
She found nothing but the cat.
" I never did see the like of that boy! "
She went to the open door and stood in it, and looked
out among the tomato vines and tall weeds that con-
stituted the garden. No Tom. So she lifted up her
voice and shouted :—
" Tom! "
There was a slight noise behind her, and she turned

just in time to seize a small boy by his belt and arrest his flight.

" There! I might have thought of that cupboard. What have you been doing in there ? "

" Nothing."

" Nothing! Look at your hands, and look at your mouth. What is that mess ? "

" I don't know, Aunt."

" Well, I know. It's jam, that's what it is. Forty times I've said that if you didn't let that jam alone I'd skin you. Hand me that switch."

The switch hovered in the air—the peril was desperate.

" My! Look behind you, Aunt! "

The old lady whirled round, and snatched her skirts out of danger. The lad fled on the instant, scrambled up the high board fence, and disappeared over it. His Aunt Polly stood surprised a moment, and then broke into a gentle laugh.

" Hang it, can't I ever learn anything ? Hasn't he played me tricks enough like that for me to be looking out for them by this time ? But my goodness, he never plays them alike two days, and how is a body to know what's coming. I'll just be obliged to make him work to-morrow, to punish him. It's mighty hard to make him work on Saturdays, when all the boys are having a holiday, but he hates work more than he hates anything else, and I've got to do some of my duty by him."

Saturday morning came and all the summer world was bright and fresh, and brimming with life. There was a song in every heart ; and if the heart was young,

the music issued at the lips. There was cheer in every
face, and a spring in every step. The locust trees were
in bloom, and the fragrance of the blossoms filled the
air. . . .

Tom appeared on the side-walk with a bucket of
whitewash and a long-handled brush. He surveyed the
fence, and the gladness went out of nature, and a deep
melancholy settled down over his spirit. Thirty yards
of fence nine feet high! It seemed to him that life was
hollow and existence but a burden. Sighing, he dipped
his brush and passed it along the topmost plank;
repeated the operation; did it again; compared the
insignificant whitewashed streak with the far-reaching
continent of unwhitewashed fence, and sat down on a
tree-box discouraged. Jim came skipping out at the
gate with a tin pail, and singing "Buffalo Gals."
Bringing water from the town pump had always been
hateful work in Tom's eyes before, but now it did not
strike him so. He remembered that there was company
at the pump. White, mulatto, and negro boys and girls
were always there waiting their turns, resting, trading
playthings, quarrelling, fighting, skylarking. And he
remembered that although the pump was only a hundred
and fifty yards away Jim never got back with a bucket
of water under an hour; and even then somebody
generally had to go after him. Tom said :—

"Say, Jim; I'll fetch the water if you'll whitewash
some."

Jim shook his head, and said :—

"Can't, Ma'rs Tom. Ole missis she tole me I got to
go an' git dis water an' not stop foolin' roun' wid

anybody. She say she spec' Ma'rs Tom gwyne to ax me to whitewash, an' so she tole me go 'long an' 'tend to ma own business—she 'lowed she'd 'tend to de whitewashin'.''

" Oh, never you mind what she said, Jim. That's the way she always talks. Gimme the bucket—I won't be gone only a minute. She won't ever know."

" Oh, I darn't, Ma'rs Tom. Ole missis she take an' tar de head off'n me. 'Deed she would."

" She! She never licks anybody—whacks 'em over the head with her thimble, and who cares for that, I'd like to know ? She talks awful, but talk don't hurt— anyways, it don't if she don't cry. Jim, I'll give you a marble. I'll give you a white alley! "

Jim began to waver.

" White alley, Jim ; and it's a bully taw."

" My ; dat's a mighty gay marbel, I tell you. But, Ma'rs Tom, I's powerful 'fraid ole missis—— "

But Jim was only human—this attraction was too much for him. He put down his pail, and took the white alley. In another minute he was flying down the street with his pail and a tingling rear, Tom was white-washing with vigour, and Aunt Polly was retiring from the field with a slipper in her hand and triumph in her eye.

But Tom's energy did not last. He began to think of the fun he had planned for this day, and his sorrows multiplied. Soon the free boys would come tripping along on all sorts of delicious expeditions, and they would make a world of fun of him for having to work— the very thought of it burnt him like fire. He got out his worldly wealth and examined it—bits of toys, marbles and trash ; enough to buy an exchange of work, maybe, but not enough to buy so much as half-an-hour of pure freedom. So he returned his straitened means to his pocket, and gave up the idea of buying the boys. At this dark and hopeless moment an inspiration burst upon him. Nothing less than a great, magnificent inspiration. He took up his brush and went tranquilly to work. Ben Rogers hove in sight presently ; the very boy of all boys whose ridicule he had been dreading. Ben's gait was the hop, skip, and jump—proof enough that his heart was light and his anticipations high. He was eating an apple, and giving a long, melodious whoop at intervals, followed by a deep-toned ding dong dong, ding dong dong, for he was impersonating a steamboat. As he drew near he slackened speed, took the middle of the street, leaned far over to starboard, and rounded-to ponderously, and with laborious pomp and circumstance, for he was impersonating the " Big Missouri," and considered himself to be drawing nine feet of water. He was boat, and captain, and engine-bells combined, so he had to imagine himself standing on his own hurricane deck giving the orders and executing them. . . .

Tom went on whitewashing—paid no attention to the steamer. Ben stared a moment, and then said :—

" Hi-yi! You're up a stump, ain't you ? "

No answer. Tom surveyed his last touch with the eye of an artist ; then he gave his brush another gentle sweep, and surveyed the result as before. Ben ranged up alongside of him. Tom's mouth watered for the apple, but he stuck to his work. Ben said :—

"Hello, old chap ; you got to work, hey ? "

"Why, it's you, Ben! I warn't noticing."

"Say, I'm going in a-swimming, I am. Don't you wish you could ? But of course you'd druther work, wouldn't you ? 'Course you would ! "

Tom contemplated the boy a bit, and said :—

"What do you call work ? "

"Why, ain't that work ? "

Tom resumed his whitewashing, and answered carelessly :—

"Well, maybe it is, and maybe it ain't. All I know is, it suits Tom Sawyer."

"Oh, come now, you don't mean to let on that you like it ? "

The brush continued to move.

"Like it ? Well, I don't see why I oughtn't to like it. Does a boy get a chance to whitewash a fence every day ? "

That put the thing in a new light. Ben stopped nibbling his apple. Tom swept his brush daintily back and forth—stepped back to note the effect—added a touch here and there—Ben watching every move, more and more absorbed. Presently he said :—

"Say, Tom, let me whitewash a little."

Tom considered ; was about to consent ; but he altered his mind :—"No, no ; I reckon it wouldn't hardly do, Ben. You see, Aunt Polly's awful particular about this fence—right here on the street, you know—but if it was the back fence, I wouldn't mind, and she wouldn't. Yes, she's awful particular about this fence ;

it's got to be done very careful ; I reckon there ain't a boy in a thousand that can do it in the way it's got to be done."

" No—is that so ? Oh, come now ; lemme just try, only just a little. I'd let you, if you was me, Tom."

" Ben, I'd like to, honest injun ; but Aunt Polly—well, Jim wanted to do it, but she wouldn't let him. If you was to tackle this fence, and anything was to happen to it—— "

" Oh, shucks ; I'll be just as careful. Now lemme try. Say—I'll give you the core of my apple."

" Well, here. No, Ben ; now don't ; I'm afeard—— "

" I'll give you the whole of it ! "

Tom gave up the brush with reluctance in his face, but alacrity in his heart. And while the late steamer " Big Missouri " worked and sweated in the sun, the retired artist sat on a barrel in the shade close by, dangled his legs, munched his apple, and planned the slaughter of more innocents. There was no lack of material ; boys happened along every little while ; they came to jeer, but remained to whitewash.

By the time Ben was fagged out, Tom had traded the next chance to Billy Fisher for a kite in good repair ; and when he played out, Johnny Miller bought in ; and so on ; and so on ; hour after hour. And when the middle of the afternoon came, from being a poor, poverty-stricken boy in the morning, Tom was literally rolling in wealth. He had, besides the things I have mentioned, twelve marbles, part of a jew's harp, a piece of blue bottle-glass to look through, a spool-cannon, a key that wouldn't unlock anything, a fragment of

chalk, a glass stopper of a decanter, a tin soldier, a couple of tadpoles, six fire-crackers, a brass door-knob, a dog-collar—but no dog—the handle of a knife, four pieces of orange-peel, and a dilapidated old window-sash. He had had a nice, good, idle time all the while —plenty of company—and the fence had three coats of whitewash on it! If he hadn't run out of whitewash. he would have bankrupted every boy in the village.

Tom said to himself that it was not such a hollow world after all. He had discovered a great law of human nature, without knowing it, namely, that, in order to make a man or a boy covet a thing, it is only necessary to make the thing difficult to attain.

From "Tom Sawyer," by Mark Twain.

INTERESTING FACTS
ABOUT
THE UNITED STATES OF AMERICA.

1. The United States of America, popularly called " The States," " U.S.A.," " The Land of Liberty," and " The Land of the Free," is a vast country stretching across the middle of North America. This country, which was at one time inhabited by Red Indians, is now the home of a " nation of nations," as people from every part of the world have gone to live in this land of wealth and promise. These settlers met, mingled, and worked with great enterprise, and, as a result of their efforts, the United States has become one of the most important countries in the world.

2. In 1620 the **Pilgrim Fathers**, a band of Puritans in England who sought freedom of worship, set forth for America in the sailing-ship **Mayflower.** Three months after leaving Plymouth Harbour, they reached the shores of what is now called New England, and founded the American township of Plymouth. Although they often had difficult times with the native Red Indian tribes, the colony soon prospered and more and more settlers joined them. The Indians used a new kind of grain, which the settlers called " **Indian corn** " (now termed maize) and they ate strange birds called

turkeys. On the last Thursday of November the Americans celebrate **Thanksgiving Day** with a feast of turkey and Indian corn.

3. A great many emigrants went from European countries to America and thirteen colonies were formed, all of them under English rule. The government in England, however, took little interest in her American colonies, except from the point of view of trade. When certain taxes and laws were ordered by the English Parliament, the colonists opposed them and the bitter feeling, as illustrated by the " **Boston Tea Party**," gradually led to war. At first the colonists fared badly, but later they rallied and eventually won final victory, under the able leadership of **George Washington**.

4. The **American Declaration of Independence** was signed on the **4th July, 1776**. This day is still celebrated as the " **birthday** " of this great nation, and is called **Independence Day**. The leaders of the new country decided they would form a **Republic**, which would have no king but would have a **President**, chosen every four years by a vote of all the people. George Washington, who had led them so successfully in the war, became the first President and was called " **The Father of the United States**."

5. The " **Americans** " dwelt in the eastern part of the country, but many of them decided to explore further inland, and settle on the rich farming land there. These pioneers travelled in **covered waggons** or **prairie schooners**, which rocked and rolled their way westward over the open, flat country. Each vehicle carried the settler's family and equipment, and was his home and

fort while on the move, a place wherein to sleep at the end of a long day's journey, and a barricade against unfriendly Indians. The **Frontier Scouts** and **Plainsmen** were the trail blazers and fighters, who gave advice and acted as escorts to the settlers when travelling in dangerous territory.

6. Shortly after the discovery of the New World by Columbus, many Spaniards travelled northward from Mexico and settled along the western coast of America. That is why many places in this region such as San Francisco, Los Angeles, Sacramento, and Santa Barbara have Spanish names. In 1849 the chance discovery of gold brought many people to California and numerous mining towns sprang up in a very short time. " **The Golden Gate** " (the channel connecting the harbour of

San Francisco with the Pacific Ocean) was so called because many of the seekers of the precious yellow metal passed this way to and from the rich gold-fields.

7. In the lower basin of the **Missouri-Mississippi** (the longest river in the U.S.A.) stretch the great **cotton plantations,** once tilled by black slaves taken forcibly from Africa, and still cultivated by negro labour. The northern states of America did not use negroes as slaves like the cotton states of the south, and they tried to stop this evil. In 1861, while **Abraham Lincoln** was President, a dreadful **Civil War** broke out. After four years of bitter fighting, the southern states were defeated and slavery was abolished. During this war the famous song, " John Brown's body lies a'mouldering in the grave," was composed and it became the marching song of the northern troops.

8. In American cities, men have erected huge

STATUE OF LIBERTY   SKYSCRAPERS   COTTONFIELD

buildings (**skyscrapers**), some as many as fifty flats high. The national capital of the United States is **Washington** and the **White House** is the home of the President. The famous **Statue of Liberty** in New York harbour was a gift from France.

The following table gives a rough idea of the value of the money used in America :—

A Cent	(1 c.)
A Nickel	(5 c.)
A Dime	(10 c.)
A Quarter	(25 c.)
A Half	(50 c.)
A Dollar	($1.00)

9. While English is the national language of the country, some immigrants have continued the manners, customs, and even the tongue of their homeland, and newspaper, in all languages, may be seen on the book-stalls.

Here are some common English words for which the Americans have different names :—sweets—candies, shop—store, motor-car—automobile, motor-lorry—truck, tram-car—street-car, pavement—side-walk, petrol—gas, lift—elevator, dust-bin—garbage-can, holiday—vacation, trousers—pants, waistcoat—vest, laces—shoe-ties, tin—can, jug—pitcher.

There are also differences in the spelling of certain words :—colour—color, honour—honor, socks—sox, through—thru, programme—program.

10. The national banner of the United States of America, commonly known as " **The Stars and Stripes** " or " **Old Glory**," is a flag bearing 50 stars and 13 stripes.

Each star represents a present-day state and each stripe stands for one of the original colonies. The national anthem is the " **Star Spangled Banner**," and the national emblems are the **eagle** and the **buffalo**. The national sport may be said to be **baseball**.

QUESTIONS ON THE STORY.

1. What was the pen-name of the author of the story ?
2. Where did Tom hide from his aunt ?
3. What was his aunt's name ?
4. Why was Tom in hiding ?
5. How did he escape immediate punishment ?
6. What kind of day was the following Saturday ?
7. What work had Tom been ordered to do ?
8. What was the little negro boy's name ?
9. On what errand had he been sent ?
10. What did Tom give him for an exchange of work ?
11. How were their plans upset ?
12. Whose ridicule had Tom been dreading most of all ?
13. What was this lad eating and at what game was he playing ?

14. How did Tom make him want to whitewash the fence ?
15. What reward did the lad offer Tom ?
16. What happened when the other boys came along ?
17. Name other boys mentioned in the story.
18. Give a list of four things which the boys traded to Tom ?
19. How many coats of whitewash did the fence receive ?
20. What law of human nature did Tom discover ?

QUESTIONS ON THE INTERESTING FACTS.

1. Give a popular name for the United States of America.
2. (*a*) Who were (1) the original natives, (2) the first white settlers ?
   (*b*) What is " Indian corn " ?
3. Who led the victorious forces of the colonists against the British ?
4. (*a*) When was the American Declaration of Independence signed ?
   (*b*) What is a Republic ?
5. (*a*) What was a " covered waggon " ?
   (*b*) Who were the (1) Frontier Scouts, (2) Plainsmen ?
6. Give three American west coast towns with Spanish names.
7. (*a*) Which is the longest river in the world ?
   (*b*) Who were employed as slave labour on the cotton plant-ations ?
   (*c*) Who was President when the American Civil War broke out ?
8. (*a*) What name is given to the huge, high buildings ?
   (*b*) What is the national capital of the United States ?
   (*c*) What famous monument stands at the entrance of New York harbour ?
9. (*a*) Name four American coins.
   (*b*) Give three common English words for which the Americans have (1) different names, (2) different spelling.
10. In the United States, what is the national (*a*) banner, (*b*) emblem, (*c*) sport?

THE FAMOUS LAKE

I N the southern part of Trinidad, about sixty miles from Port of Spain, lies a lake which is famed throughout the world. Though some of its surface is a drab expanse of asphalt it is, nevertheless, a lake. It has water and fishes and, until a few years ago, there were some alligators in it too. If we started to walk over the lake, we should have to wade sometimes through deep pools, and be very careful not to step on one of the soft spots where the asphalt has not yet hardened, or we should stick fast. Coarse scrub and a few trees grow on the sloping banks around the lake, and there are a few little islands with similar vegetation on the lake itself. The only birds to be seen are ugly, black vultures, known locally as korbos.

How was this remarkable lake formed? Thousands of years ago heavy, sticky oil started to bubble up through the bed of the lake from prehistoric rocks far below. This oily substance stayed on the bottom of the lake and mixed with the sandy sediment there. The mixing process was helped by the presence of gases whose movement stirred the sediment gently. Through the ages more oil seeped in, and the gentle churning process went on, until much of the lake was a thick emulsion which hardened when exposed to air.

The earliest description of the lake is that which Sir Walter Raleigh wrote in his diary after visiting Trinidad in 1617. Here is a part of it :

" . . . a piece of land of some 2 leagues long and a league broad, all of stone pitch or bitumen which rises out of the ground in little springs or fountains and

so running a little way, it hardens in the air and covers all the plain. There are also many springs of water and in and among them fresh water fish.''

It was natural that Raleigh viewed the lake as a plain for at that time none of the asphalt had been removed, and it spread over a surface far beyond the actual basin of the lake. Raleigh's ships, like all other ships at that time, were made of wood, and he found the asphalt very useful for caulking the seams to make the ships watertight.

Men discovered, long ago, that asphalt had very strong binding qualities. In Mesopotamia, 5,000 years ago, it was used in building to hold the bricks together. Perhaps the Babylonians used it when building that great tower which they hoped would reach the sky. The asphalt used by these early builders was found in rock form in countries around the Mediterranean Sea. It is still mined in this form in Switzerland, France, Sicily and Germany. Only Trinidad has a lake of asphalt.

In the early part of the 19th century attempts were made to use the lake asphalt for various purposes. People tried to burn it as fuel, but this was not a success. Then they tried to extract the oil for use in lamps but, of course, it was not the right kind of oil for that. Strangely enough, the first experiment in the use of the lake asphalt for road-making was also unsuccessful. In 1815 Sir Ralph Woodward, who was then governor of Trinidad, was concerned at the rapid growth of weeds in the streets of Port of Spain. He decided that a layer of asphalt would kill the weeds and give a good road surface. The work was carried out but, instead of dying off, the weeds grew more luxuriantly than before. Probably the ground had been dug too deeply before the asphalt was applied, and the coating given was too thin. Experiments in refining the asphalt to make it suitable for pavements and roads continued, however, and in 1870 the first Trinidad asphalt pavement was laid in Newark, New Jersey, U.S.A. By the end of the 19th century great quantities of asphalt were being dug out of the lake to be shipped to many oversea countries for use in road-making.

DIGGING OUT THE ASPHALT

Trinidad asphalt is of good quality because it contains a high proportion of bitumen. It is also fairly easily obtained, although constant pumping must be carried on to drain off the water from the lake. Until recent years the asphalt was dug out by men working in small gangs and using specially designed pick-axes. One man did the digging and four or five others carried the huge chunks of asphalt, some of them weighing 100 lbs., on their heads to the tramway which took them to the lakeside.

Nowadays, mechanical diggers break the asphalt into small pieces and tip them into a nearby truck. The diggers remove the asphalt to a depth of three feet. As soon as this top crust is removed, liquid asphalt starts flowing in to fill up the trench, and in two or three weeks the area is ready for digging again. Duck-boards have to be laid down before the mechanical diggers go on to the lake as otherwise the danger of sinking in is great.

REFINING

The material when dug out of the lake is called crude asphalt for it contains some water and gas as well as pieces of wood and other vegetable matter. To make it suitable for road-making and other purposes it must be purified. At the refinery on the lakeside are a number of rectangular steel tanks fitted with steam coils. Each tank can take 120 tons of crude asphalt. When the tank is loaded, a considerable pressure of hot, wet steam is released to blow through the contents. This process usually goes on for about eight hours before the gas and water are driven off. Then the now liquid asphalt is strained twice through perforated metal plates or cylinders, when it is ready for filling into fibre-board containers. When the containers have cooled they are transported by overhead cable to the pier to await shipment to oversea countries.

WHAT ASPHALT IS USED FOR

The most important use of asphalt is undoubtedly for road-surfacing. The roads of practically every country in the world today are crowded with motor vehicles of all kinds, from mini-cars to heavy haulage trucks. Good roads are therefore essential for safety and comfort. They must be smooth but not slippery, hard-wearing, and capable of withstanding great pressure. Asphalt, mixed with stone chips, gives the required surface for modern roads. Where rock asphalt is used it has been found that the addition of a proportion of lake asphalt gives a longer life to the road, and prevents it becoming slippery.

Surprisingly, too, many roofs are now made of a

cement mixture which contains asphalt. Such material is durable, thoroughly waterproof, and does not corrode. The famous Tate Gallery in London is only one of many buildings in Britain's capital city which has some lake asphalt in its roof. Indeed, there are few countries in the world in which one would not find some use being made of asphalt from the famous lake in Trinidad.

QUESTIONS ON THE STORY

1. Where is the famous lake?
2. Can you tell how the lake was formed?
3. What did Sir Walter Raleigh use the lake asphalt for?
4. Asphalt was used in building in Old Testament times. What was the name of the high tower we hear of in the Bible?
5. Was the first asphalt road laid in Port of Spain a success? Explain what happened.
6. (a) How was asphalt formerly dug from the lake?
   (b) How is it dug out now?
7. How is the asphalt refined or purified?
8. Why are good roads so important nowadays?
9. What makes the best surface for modern roads?
10. What famous building in London has lake asphalt in its roof?

"THE CHRISTIANS TO THE LIONS"

(At the time of this story, the Roman idea of sport was to watch dangerous chariot races, gladiators fighting duels to the death, wild animals tearing each other to pieces, and the sacrifice of helpless, unarmed people who did not believe in the Roman gods. The Colosseum was the large building in which most of these blood-thirsty shows were staged.)

THERE was great excitement in the Colosseum, for it was known that the Emperor Nero had given orders that some of the condemned Christians should be given to the lions. There was a hush of expectancy as the door of a dungeon was opened, and there entered a procession, consisting of a priest of Jupiter and several attendants of the temple, followed by four guards conducting an elderly man with his two sons, lads of seventeen or eighteen.

They made their way across the arena, and stopped before the emperor. The priest approached the prisoners, holding out a small image of the god, and offered them their lives if they would worship it. All refused. They were then conducted back to the centre of the arena, and the attendants, leaving them there, filed out through the door.

The old man laid his hands on the shoulders of his sons and began singing a hymn, in which they both joined. Their voices rose loud and clear in the silence of the amphitheatre, and there was neither pause nor waver in the tone as the entrance to one of the cages at the other end of the arena was opened, and a lion and a lioness appeared.

The animals stood hesitating as they looked around at the sea of faces; then, encouraged by the silence, they stepped out, and, side by side, made the circuit of the arena. When they had completed the circle, they again paused, and now, for the first time, turned their attention to the three figures standing in its centre. For a minute they stood irresolute, and then, crouching low, crawled towards the old man and his sons.

The spectators shuddered. Among them was Beric, a brave British lad, who had been brought a captive to Rome, and had been trained to be a gladiator by Scopus, a noted swordsman. He could view, without emotion, a contest of armed men, but he could not, like the population of Rome, see unarmed and unresisting men pulled down by wild beasts.

There was now a dead silence in the crowded amphitheatre, broken at last by a low sound as of a gasping breath. One voice alone continued the hymn, and soon that too suddenly ceased. The tragedy was over, and the buzz of conversation and comment again broke out among the spectators. Certainly these Christians knew how to die.

A strong body of guards, provided with torches, entered. The lions were driven back to their dens, the bodies being left where they had fallen. Four batches of prisoners who were brought out, one after another, met with a similar fate. Then there was another pause. It was known that a girl of noble family was to be the last victim.

Again the doors opened. A priest of Diana headed a procession of white-robed attendants, and six virgins from the temple of Diana entered, followed by Ennia in the midst of a band of lictors. Even the hardened hearts of the spectators were moved by the youth and beauty of the young girl, who, dressed in white, advanced calmly between her guards, with a gentle, modest expression on her features.

When the procession formed up before the emperor, she saluted him. The priest and the virgins surrounded her, and urged her to pay reverence to the statue of Diana. Pointing to her parents, they implored her for their sake to recant. Pale as death, and with tears streaming down her cheeks, she shook her head slowly. " I cannot deny the Lord who died for me," she said.

Nero himself rose from his seat. " Maiden," he said, " if not for your own sake, then for the sake of those who love you, I pray you to cease from your obstinacy. How can a child like you know more than the wisest heads of Rome ? How can you deny the gods who have protected and given victory to your country ? I would fain spare you."

" I am but a child as you say, Caesar," Ennia replied. " I have no strength of my own, but I am strong in the strength of Him I worship. He gave His life for me ; it is not much that I should give mine for Him."

Nero sank back in his seat with an angry wave of his hand. He saw that the sympathy of the audience was with the prisoner, and would willingly have gained their approval by extending his clemency towards her. The procession now returned to the centre of the arena, where the girls, weeping, took leave of Ennia, who soon stood alone, a slight, helpless figure, in the sight of the great silent multitude.

Nero had spoken in a low tone to one of his attendants. The door of another cage was opened, and a lion larger than any that had previously entered the arena, saluted the spectators with a deep roar. As it did so, a tall figure, clad in a tunic, sprang forward from a group of attendants behind a strong barrier at the other end of the arena. It was Beric the Briton. He was armed only with a sword, which he had snatched from a soldier standing next to him.

A burst of applause rose from the spectators. This was a novelty, and an excitement beyond what they had bargained for. They had been moved by the youth of the victim, and now the prospects of something more exciting than the rending to pieces of a defenceless girl enlisted them in favour of her champion. Moreover, the Romans intensely admired feats of bravery, and that this captive should offer to face, single-handed, an animal that was known to be the most powerful of those in the amphitheatre, filled them with admiration.

Accustomed as they were to gaze at athletes, they were struck with the physique and strength of the young Briton, whose muscles stood up massive and knotted through the white skin. " Let him fight ! " they shouted ; " let him fight ! "

Nero waited till the acclamation ceased, then ordered the lion to be driven back to its den, and said : " The people have spoken ; let their will be done. But we must not be unfair to the lion ; as the maiden was unarmed, so shall you stand unarmed before the lion."

The decision was received in silence by the spectators. It seemed a sentence of death to the young Briton, and the silence was succeeded by a low murmur of disapproval. Beric turned a little pale, but showed no other sign of emotion.

" I accept the conditions," he said in a loud steady voice, " it being understood that should I conquer, the damsel shall be free from all penalty, and shall be restored to her parents."

" That is understood," Nero replied.

With an inclination of his head to the emperor, and a wave of his hand to the spectators, Beric turned and walked across the arena to where his friend Scopus awaited him with a cloak. Wrapping himself in its ample folds, he walked to the centre of the arena. A murmur of surprise arose. Why should the Briton cumber his limbs with this garment ?

Throwing off the cloak, he exclaimed, " You see I am unarmed. I have not so much as a dagger." Then tearing off two broad strips from the edge of the garment, he twisted them into ropes, and formed a running noose in each. What was left of the cloak he threw over his arm, and signed to the attendants at the cage to open the door.

" Oh, Beric ! Why have you thrown away your life

in a useless attempt to save mine? Ennia asked, as he stood before her.

" It may not be useless, Ennia. God has protected me through many dangers, and He will surely assist me now. Pray to Him for aid."

The door of the den opened. Beric stepped a few paces towards it. The spectators cheered. They had understood his purpose in making the ropes—that he was to use his cloak as a retiarius used his net. There was to be a contest then, not a mere slaughter. The lion dashed out of its den with a sudden spring, made three or four leaps forward, and then paused with its eyes fixed on the lad standing in front of it, still and immovable, in an easy pose, ready for action.

Then it sank till its body nearly touched the ground, and began to crawl with a stealthy gliding motion towards him. More and more slowly it went, till it paused at a distance of some ten yards. For a few seconds it crouched motionless, save for a slow, waving movement of its tail ; then, with a sharp roar, it sprang through the air. With a motion as quick Beric leaped aside.

As it touched the ground, he sprang across its loins and wrapped his cloak in many folds round its head, knotting the ends tightly. Then, as the lion, recovering from its first surprise, sprang to its feet with a roar of anger and disgust, Beric was on his feet beside it. For a moment it strove to tear the strange substance which enveloped its head. But Beric dropped the end of a noose over one of its forepaws, drew it tight, and with a sudden pull jerked the animal over on to its back.

As it sprang up again the other forepaw was noosed, and it was again thrown over. This time, as it sprang to its feet, Beric struck it a heavy blow on the nose. The unexpected assault brought it down for a moment, but mad with rage it sprang up and struck out in all directions at its invisible foe, leaping and bounding hither and thither. Beric easily avoided the onslaught, and taking every opportunity, struck it three or four times with all his force on the ear, each time rolling it over and over.

246

The last of these blows seemed to stun it, and it lay for a moment motionless. Again Beric leaped upon it, coming down astride of its loins with all his weight, and seizing at once the two ropes. The lion uttered a roar of dismay and pain, and struck at him first with one paw, and then with the other. By his coolness and quickness, however, he escaped all the blows, and when the lion seemed exhausted, he jerked tightly the cords, twisting them behind the lion's back, and with rapid turns fastening them together.

The lion was helpless now. As it rolled over and over, uttering roars of vain fury, Beric snatched the cloth from its head, tore off another strip, twisted it, and without difficulty bound its hind-legs together. Then he again wrapped it round the lion's head, and stood up, breathless but victorious. A mighty shout shook the building. Never had such a feat been seen in the arena before. Men and women rose from their seats and waved their hands in frantic enthusiasm.

Beric had not escaped altogether unhurt. As the lion had struck out at him, it had torn away a piece of flesh from his side, and the blood was streaming down over his white tunic. He now went up to Ennia, who was standing with closed eyes and hands clasped in prayer. She had seen nothing of the conflict, and had believed that Beric's death and her own were inevitable.

" Ennia," he said, " God has saved us ; the lion is helpless now." And with these words he led her forth from the place that had been for both the very jaws of death.

From "Beric the Briton," by G. A. Henty.

THE ORIGIN OF OUR ALPHABET

THE word **Alphabet** is derived from the names of the first two letters in Greek (alpha, beta), and is the term applied to the collection of letters which make up the words of a language.

When primitive peoples wished to convey ideas to others by another means than speech, they did so by scratching rough drawings or pictures on wood, or stone, or some other suitable substance. The oldest alphabets were therefore **Pictographs**—picture signs denoting certain things.

The modern English alphabet can be traced to the Roman member of Latin alphabets and English printed letters are still called Roman type.

	PICTOGRAPHS		PHOENICIAN	ANCIENT GREEK		GREEK	EARLY LATIN	ROMAN		MODERN ENGLISH	
1	OX	∠	⋉	△		A	A	A	a	A	a a
2	HOUSE	⊔⊔	⇘	⧖		B	ß	B	b	B b	ℓ
3	CAMEL	∧	⟩	7		Γ	⟨	C	{ C / G g	C c	∘
4	DOOR	◻	△	△	REVERSED.	△	▷	D	d	D d	d
5	MAN	ⴹ	⟋	⟋		E	ε	E	e	E e	∘
6	HOOK	⅄	⅄	⅄	ARE	F	ꜰ	F	f	F f	ƒ
7					LETTERS					G g	ɠ
8	FENCE	⧻	目	日	THE	H	ʜ	H	h	H h	ₕ
9	FINGER	⎰	⅂	⎰	OF	I	ǀ	I	{ ǀ / ǀǀ	I i	∘
10					MANY					J j	ⱼ
11	PALM BRANCH	⅄	⅄	⅄	GREEK	K	ᴋ	K	k	K k	ₖ
12	OX WHIP	∧	∟	✓	ANCIENT	∧	ᴌ	L	l	L l	ℓ
13	WATER	∿	⋏	⋎		M	ᴍ	M	m	M m	ₘ
14	SNAKE	∽	⋏	⋌	AFTER	N	ᴎ	N	n	N n	ₙ
15	EYE	⊙	○	○	THAT	O	○	O	o	O o	∘
16	FISH HOOK	?	?	⁊	NOTE	Γ	ᴘ	P	p	P p	ₚ
17	MOUTH	⊖	Φ	Φ		Φ	Ϙ	Q	q	Q q	ɋ
18	HEAD	○	△	△		P	ᴙ	R	r	R r	ᵣ
19	TOOTH	⩊	W	⧢		Ϟ	ᔑ	S	sf	S s	∘
20	CROSS	✝	✝	Τ		T	ᴛ	T	t	T t	ₜ
21							{ U	U	u	U u	ⱶ
22						∨	V	V	v	V v	ᵥ
23								W	w	W w	ᵥᵥ
24	TREE	⩱	⩲	⩲		⩴	X	X	x	X x	∞
25				⅄		⅄		Y	y	Y y	ᵧ
26	OLIVE TWIG	⊬	⧧	⧧		Z		Z	z	Z z	ȝ

THE FACE OF THE EARTH

GEOGRAPHY is the study of the surface of the earth and its inhabitants.

ATMOSPHERE - the air surrounding the earth.

AVALANCHE - a mass of snow, ice, or rocks sliding down a mountain.

BAY - - - an inlet of the sea—sometimes called a gulf.

CANAL - - a waterway constructed by man.

CAPE - - - a point of land stretching out into the sea. Other names are **bill butt, foreland head mull naze ness,** promontory, and **point.**

CHANNEL -   - a narrow portion of water joining two large stretches of water, and sometimes called a **strait.**

CLIFF -   -   - the steep face of a mountain or rocky sea-shore.

CLIMATE -   - the weather conditions.

COAST   -   - land washed by the sea—sometimes called **shore** ; if flat or sandy— **seaside** or **beach.**

CONTINENT   - a large stretch of land not broken up by seas.

COUNTRY -   - an area of land under one government.

CREEK   -   - a small inlet of the sea—a **cove.** In America and Australia a creek is a small river.

DESERT   -   - a bare stretch of land—a **wilderness.**

EQUATOR -   - an imaginary line round the earth, midway between the North and South Poles.

GLACIER -   - a river of ice moving very slowly down the slope of a mountain.

HARBOUR -   - an inlet of the sea where ships can shelter—sometimes called a **haven.**

HILL -   -   - a mass of high land ; if very high it is called a **ben, mountain** or **peak.** Several mountains together form a **group** ; connected mountains form a **chain** or **range.**

HORIZON -   - the line where earth and sky seem to meet.

Iceberg - -	a floating mountain of ice ; a field of floating ice is termed an **ice-floe**.
Island - -	a portion of land completely surrounded by water.
Isthmus - -	a narrow neck of land joining two larger stretches of land.
Lake - - -	a stretch of water surrounded by land. Sometimes it is called a **mere** ; if very small—a **pool** ; if in high lands —a **tarn** ; if filled with sea-water— a **lagoon**. In Scotland a lake is called a **loch** ; in Ireland, a **lough**.
Latitude -	the distance north or south of the equator.
Longitude	the distance east or west of a line which passes through Greenwich, London, from North Pole to South Pole.
Oasis - - -	a fertile spot in the desert affording water and shelter.
Ocean -	a vast stretch of water ; a smaller stretch is called a **sea**.
Peninsula	a piece of land almost surrounded by water.
Plain -	a level piece of land ; if wet called a **bog, fen**, or **marsh** ; if untilled, a **heath** or **moor** ; if at a high level, a **plateau** or **tableland**. Wide regions of fairly level ground in each of the continents have acquired special names such as the **Steppes** and **Tundras** of eastern Europe and

Asia ; the **Deserts** of Arabia and Africa ; the **Savannahs** and **Prairies** of North America ; the **Llanos, Pampas,** and **Selvas** of South America.

POLAR REGIONS   the cold parts of the earth near the North and South Poles.

RIVER - - a stream of fresh water flowing into a lake or sea. The beginning is called the **source** or **spring** ; the sides— its **banks** ; little streams which flow into it—**feeders** or **tributaries** ; where the water lies—its **bed** ; the land it drains—its **basin** ; the direction it takes—its **course**. The end of a river is its **mouth,** but if very wide—its **estuary** or **firth**. If the river enters the sea by two or more branches, the mouth is known as a **delta**. A very small river is called a **brook, burn, rivulet,** or **streamlet**.

SHIRE - - a part or division of a country. Other names are **canton, county, department,** and **state**.

TROPICS - - the hot region of the earth near the equator.

VALLEY - - low land with hills on either side. Other names are **dale, glen, strath,** and **vale**. If the valley has very steep sides it is called a **canyon, gorge,** or **ravine**.

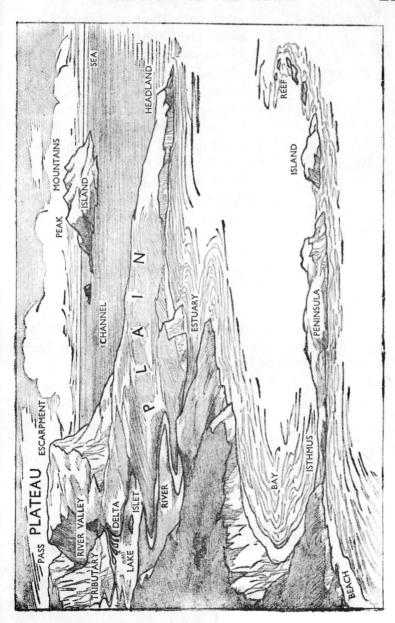

VOLCANO - - - an opening in the earth's surface from which lava, hot ashes, molten earth and steam pour out.

WATERFALL - where water of a river falls from a higher to a lower level ; if very large it is called a **cataract** ; if the bed of the river slopes causing the water to flow swiftly—a **rapid**.

WIND - .- - air in motion. Here are the various names of the wind, ranging from the lightest to the strongest :—

Zephyr or **Light**
  Breeze - - 2 to 12 m.p.h.
Moderate Wind - 13 to 23 m.p.h.
Strong Wind - 24 to 37 m.p.h.
Gale - - - 38 to 55 m.p.h.
Storm - - - 56 to 75 m.p.h.
Hurricane - - Above 75 m.p.h.

A violent hurricane in the China Seas is called a **typhoon**. If the wind moves with a circular motion it is called a **cyclone** or whirlwind.